Wealth, Trade, Prices, and Money

I0504379

A Storyteller's Little Book of Economic Theory

WEALTH, TRADE, PRICES, AND MONEY

A Storyteller's Little Book of Economic Theory

ROBERT L. GREENFIELD
Fairleigh Dickinson University

iUniverse, Inc.
New York   Bloomington

Wealth, Trade, Prices, and Money
A Storyteller's Little Book of Economic Theory
Copyright © 2006, 2007, 2008 by Robert L. Greenfield

All rights reserved. No part of this book may be used or reproduced by any means, graphic, electronic, or mechanical, including photocopying, recording, taping or by any information storage retrieval system without the written permission of the publisher except in the case of brief quotations embodied in critical articles and reviews.

iUniverse books may be ordered through booksellers or by contacting:
iUniverse
1663 Liberty Drive
Bloomington, IN 47403
www.iuniverse.com
1-800-Authors (1-800-288-4677)

Because of the dynamic nature of the Internet, any Web addresses or links contained in this book may have changed since publication and may no longer be valid. The views expressed in this work are solely those of the author and do not necessarily reflect the views of the publisher, and the publisher hereby disclaims any responsibility for them.

ISBN: 978-0-595-40900-6 (pbk)
ISBN: 978-0-595-85263-5 (ebk)

Printed in the United States of America

iUniverse rev. date: 8/31/2009

For Nancy, who knows these stories almost by heart.

Contents

Preface

From the thirty years (nearly forty years if I count my own days as a student) that I've spent in a college classroom, one lesson emerges with special clarity. Whoever said "Everyone likes a good story" had it right. And what teacher doesn't have at least a *few* good stories to tell? It doesn't take a Will Rogers or a Garrison Keillor to make storytelling work.

In this little book, I've tried to put on paper the stories that I tell in teaching a one-semester economics course, sometimes for undergraduates and sometimes for beginning M.B.A. students. When these students come to the course, they arrive with no background whatsoever in economics and, usually, with much apprehension about the subject itself. Telling stories, especially when they're personal stories or stories familiar in a different context, goes a long way toward alleviating that apprehension; the lessons become easier to learn.

As for the lessons themselves…. Well, they range from understanding how a trade deficit can enrich a nation to seeing how prices act as buffers of civility—from seeing the economy as a unified system to recognizing money's special role as the system's lubricant—from recognizing saving's fundamentally benign nature to appreciating the advantages of defining the "dollar" as something other than a piece of paper (or, for that matter, even gold) money. Some of the lessons come in historical themes— the Great Depression, World War II, and, through an allegorical interpretation of the *Wizard of Oz*, the 1890s political battle over the monetary standard; others as storylines from television programs that were popular when I was a boy (they were in "living" black and white, of course, not color); still others courtesy of my grandfather, former students, even shoppers at a local supermarket.

Naturally, the proof of the writing is in the reading. These stories seem to have worked well in person, and I'm hopeful, even optimistic, about their working well on paper, too.

1
Money Doesn't Make a Country Rich

Opening Night

Twenty unfamiliar faces…perhaps even twenty-five. "It all starts," I tell the new recruits, "with Adam Smith"; and though new to this forbidding subject called "economics", more than a few of them nod agreeably. They've heard the name. Adam Smith, after all, is perhaps the most famous economist we've ever had and his *An Inquiry into the Nature and Causes of the Wealth of Nations*, published in 1776, the most famous book. Breaking from the accepted wisdom of its age, this great work shifted attention away from money as the measure of a nation's wealth and towards the truer measure instead, goods.

Now, when stated in plain language, Adam Smith's proposition concerning a nation's wealth—that what really matters are goods, not money—might not even seem to be a disputable point. Especially in matters concerning national accounting for international trade, however, long-established terminological conventions can obscure the economic fundamentals. Here, in my first story, using some classroom theatrics, I try to lay bare those fundamentals.

The World Divided

To get things underway, I divide the class right down the middle. The half to my right becomes the United States. The half to my left becomes the rest of the world, which I call "Japan". I give one of the "Americans" a bushel of wheat (well, actually, it's only a bagel). Someone in "Japan" gets a pile of beige paper slips—Japanese money, yen.

I ask the American to sell the bagel to a fellow American and to ask $1 for it. The script calls for silence on the American side of the room,

1

however, and that's exactly what, as this production's director, I've made sure the bagel peddler gets—silence, no takers among the Americans.

"Try Japan," I advise.

But the American bagel peddler wants to know something first. "What's a dollar worth in yen?" It's a perfectly reasonable question that he asks. After all, the Japanese do business in yen, not dollars. How can the American put a yen price tag on the $1 bagel before knowing the rate at which he can exchange yen for dollars? I answer the question by saying that somebody with a dollar to sell can get 100 yen for it. Then, for that number of yen, the American offers the bagel to the other side of the room, the side that I'm calling "Japan".

On the Japanese side of the room, I've designated someone to play the bagel importer. The importer has already had a look at the script, and he knows his line. "I'll take it," the importer says, right on cue. The importer takes the bagel and, as the script requires, gives the American exporter 100 yen.

"Now what?" I ask the American exporter. "The yen won't do you much good here in the United States. You can't spend yen on this side of the room."

"Then I guess that I'll have to sell them."

The script says that the American will find no takers, however, not at the 100 yen per dollar price, anyway.

"What now?" I ask.

"I'll have to cut the price," the American answers. "What else can I do? I'll have to take less than one dollar for my 100 yen."

"Okay, then. Give it a try."

He does give it a try, now offering the 100 yen for $.90. But, still, the American finds no one who wants to buy the yen, not even at the reduced price.

The American Exporter's Uncle Sam

Now, playing the U.S. government, the American exporter's Uncle Sam, I make my own acting debut.

"You have yen to sell?" I ask the American exporter. "I'll take them, all 100 of them."

"What'll you give me for them?" the exporter wants to know.

"One dollar."

"Great!" the exporter says. He has already seen that he can't do even that well elsewhere. "It's a deal."

Yes, it's a deal, and for the Japanese a pretty good deal, too. I take out a green sheet of paper and a pair of scissors. After cutting the sheet into small rectangular pieces and marking each piece "one dollar", I give the American exporter one of the pieces. The exporter gives me the 100 yen. Then, though perhaps a bit too dramatically I've been told, I walk across the room. When I get to the wastepaper basket, I shred the yen, and then I throw them away.

"Why are you throwing them away?" my audience wants to know.

"Why not? What else am I going to do with them?"

"Buy something from Japan," they answer, almost in unison. Even *I* should understand that.

"But I'm playing the U.S. government," I remind them. "If I had wanted to buy goods, I could have bought the goods right here, in America, with the very dollars that I printed to buy the exporter's yen. I wouldn't have needed the yen in the first place. I bought the yen not because I wanted to buy Japanese goods but because I wanted to keep the dollar price of the yen from falling; American exporters didn't want their goods to become more expensive for Japanese importers."

Still, I get resistance. "Okay," I say. "Let's see what happens when I *don't* buy the yen."

I tell the story again…from the beginning. An American exporter sells his $1 bushel of wheat to a Japanese importer, in payment for the wheat takes 100 yen, and then, at the going 100 yen per dollar exchange rate, tries to sell the yen. Having trouble selling the yen, the American exporter cuts his asking price. At *some* lower dollar price, the American exporter finds a private buyer for the yen. The buyer of the yen, everyone sees, is someone who wants to import something, perhaps a car, from Japan. A cheaper yen means a cheaper Toyota, cheaper in dollars. An American buys the yen and then sends them back to Japan, in exchange for a new car or, perhaps, ownership shares in the company that produces cars.

If the government stays out of the picture, each side gets something— the Japanese, an American bagel—the Americans, a Japanese car. But if the U.S. government intervenes to buy yen and the yen wind up in the wastepaper basket (or even in an account that the Japanese government maintains for it), they don't get the chance to go back home. No American gets a chance to present the yen *as a claim against Japanese goods.* The Japanese people get the bagel; the Americans get the newly printed green paper. From the Americans' point of view, that's not a very good deal at all.

Oh sure, the American exporter is better off. From the U.S. government, after all, the American exporter gets more dollars as payment per 100 yen than he can get from anyone else, and with the new dollars, he can buy things. The American exporter can buy things, true, *but only from other Americans.* The Americans together, as a group, therefore, are poorer than they were before. The Japanese have the bagel, and for all their work producing the bagel, the Americans have the paper dollars—inedible paper dollars.

The Poverty of a "Surplus"

A country that exports goods worth more than the goods that it imports runs a trade surplus in its balance of payments. The American side of the room, therefore, has run the trade surplus; and for my listeners, this one phrase, the phrase "American trade surplus", causes doubt.

"How can a trade surplus make the country that's running it poorer?" they want to know. "A trade surplus is a good thing; isn't it?"

"But what do you have a surplus of?" I ask them. "The surplus, in this case, is a surplus of your own currency, mere pictures of deceased American dignitaries." Playing the U.S. government, I just printed the pictures into existence when I bought the American exporter's yen. In my possession, the yen are unusable claims on Japanese goods. If, for the yen that he earns by giving up his goods, the American exporter gets from the U.S. government freshly printed claims on goods that his *fellow Americans* have produced, then they are the losers. For their goods and all the work that they put into producing them, what do *they* get? They as a group get the paper dollars, but nothing else. Call the new dollars that the American government gives the exporter for the yen a "surplus"; call them anything you want to call them. But the bagel is gone, and in America, there is nothing except green paper money to take its place.

"What about your trade deficit?" I ask the Japanese side of the room. "If you're smart," I say, answering my own question even before the Japanese themselves get a chance to answer it, "you won't fret at all about it. Sure, you've lost money, literally lost it; the yen are sitting, shredded, in the American government's wastepaper basket (or, again, sitting in the U.S. government's yen account). So what? You have the bagel."

Much more clearly than anyone before him, Adam Smith understood, or at least explained, that a country whose labor yields nothing but more and more money works hard but goes hungry. Money is just paper, Adam Smith would say, and you can't eat paper. The bagel, however, is wealth, and in my story the Japanese get it for nothing because, by buying yen that the Japanese have already used to pay for the bagel, the U.S. government keeps Americans from using those hard earned yen to buy Japanese cars.

The $164 Billion Question

But why should any government intercept hard earned foreign exchange that its citizenry would otherwise use to acquire goods from other countries? Why in just three quarters of 2004 did *Asian* governments, for example, buy 164 billion dollars from their countries' exporters and, by so doing, prevent everyday Asians from using those dollars to acquire, say, American wheat? That, for the first three quarters of 2004, was the $164 billion question. It's true that, instead of just holding the dollars, the Asian governments used them to buy U.S. government bonds.[1] Still, 164 billion dollars is a lot of "Toyotas", even if only on loan, a loan that, thanks to their own governments, the Asian citizenries had no choice but to make us.

The war in Iraq might go part of the way toward answering this question. To the American-led expedition in Iraq, several Asian governments have given their verbal support. They've not to any significant extent, however, actually provided the expedition military support—Japan, not at all, because its constitution, written in the aftermath of WWII, forbids doing so.[2] Fighting a war requires more, much more, however, than just

---

1 For foreign official agencies' holdings of U.S. government bonds, see U.S. Treasury Bulletin, Table IFS2
2 The 600 Japanese soldiers in Iraq have provided humanitarian assistance, and even this assignment has caused much controversy.

putting combat troops on the ground. Fighting a war requires provisioning those troops. And from abroad, thanks to these Asian governments and their intervening in the foreign exchange market to buy dollars, the United States in the first three quarters of 2004 received $164 billion worth of provisions.

Here, in late 2004, the dollar's foreign-exchange value has dropped sharply. The sharp drop of the dollar's foreign-exchange value may mean that the Asian governments have had their fill of dollar assets. If so, then we Americans will have to pay our own way—and pay it, as they say, up front. We won't be able to deploy resources abroad *and* continue living in the style that we've become accustomed to.

2

The Mirage We Call "Foreign Competition"

Radio Days

I learned something very important that spring day, back in May 1983. When I turned on the car radio, I picked up an unexpected but familiar voice, economist Milton Friedman's voice, in an ABC radio network interview. A few minutes later, a telephone caller asked a question. The caller's question presupposed Friedman's taking for granted that American manufacturers of automobiles were actually in direct competition with foreign manufacturers. Friedman rejected the question's seemingly plausible presupposition—in fact, rejected it outright. To explain why he rejected it, Friedman recast in almost impossible-to-misunderstand terms the free trade argument of David Ricardo, whose *Principles of Political Economy and Taxation* appeared in 1817.[1]

A Virtual Car

We here in America, Friedman explained, actually have two ways of producing cars. We can do it directly, by running an assembly line in Detroit, or we can do it indirectly, by producing Kansas wheat— Kansas wheat that, when exported, pays for imported cars. The land, labor, and machines that produce just one car in Detroit might, if used in the wheat fields of Kansas, actually "produce" two foreign cars. If so, then those

---

1 In *The Armchair Economist* (Free Press, 1993), Steven Landsburg tells a story very similar to mine. He gives credit not to Milton Friedman but to his son, David Friedman.

7

American resources depart Detroit and head west for Kansas. There, right there in the wheat fields of Kansas and without an assembly line anywhere in sight, Americans produce cars.

The much vilified "foreign competition", Friedman helped me see, isn't really *foreign* competition at all. For us here in America, all competition is, in fact, domestic competition—domestic competition for scarce American resources. At its most basic level, competition in the automobile industry doesn't pit Detroit against, say, Japan; competition in the automobile industry pits Detroit against Kansas. A Japanese car's having a lower dollar price than a comparable American car has means that indirectly, through international trade, farmers in Kansas can produce a larger number of those cars than they could have produced directly, as assembly-line workers back in Detroit. America, as Friedman said, has its comparative advantage in wheat.

Injury but, Please, No Insult

An American industry's losing business, then, even though that business may outwardly seem to be going abroad, doesn't necessarily mean that the American industry is inefficient by comparison to its foreign counterpart. Detroit's car producers, for example, despite their declining business fortunes, might actually be *more* efficient than Japan's car producers are. American car producers, that is, might actually turn land, labor, and capital into more cars than the Japanese car producers do. From the American point of view, however, that particular comparison is entirely irrelevant, and it's just as irrelevant from the Japanese point of view.

The relevant question is, very simply, where does a country best use its own scarce resources—in the American case, for example, Detroit or Kansas? If the answer to the question is "Kansas", then we should be especially careful not to let anyone add verbal insult to Detroit's economic injury. Having to pack up and head off to Kansas is bad enough. Irrelevant and perhaps even inaccurate efficiency comparisons with foreign producers do nothing but make things worse for people who, en route to Kansas, are already suffering. It's a hard enough trip to "Kansas", as anyone who has had to retrain for a career change will probably attest.

Cheap Foreign Land

On the long, hard road to Kansas, of course, people will do a lot of grumbling about "cheap foreign labor" and its being the *real* cause of Detroit's problem. Cheap Asian labor poses no more a problem for Americans who really don't want to leave Detroit and move to Kansas, however, than cheap American land poses for Asians who really don't want to leave their farms and move to Asian automobile plants. Labor is probably the most abundant Asian resource, and land probably the most abundant American resource. Their abundance helps make both of them cheap. Their being cheap gives Americans who never even enter an automobile plant reason to "produce" cars and Asians who never even set eyes on a plow reason to "produce" wheat.

No one consciously decides, of course, not on behalf of the nation as a whole, anyway, to transfer American resources from Detroit's assembly lines to the wheat fields of Kansas. Nor does any one person decide, on behalf of the Asian country as a whole, to move that country's resources from agriculture to manufacturing automobiles. Resources move, yes indeed, but they move as if guided by an invisible hand, to use Adam Smith's famous phrase. The American wheat industry, America's virtual automobile industry, does a better job transforming American resources into automobiles than Detroit does, and the Asian automobile industry, Asia's virtual agricultural industry, does a better job transforming Asian resources into wheat than Asian farmers do. Both the American and Japanese virtual industries pay better than their reality counterparts could pay, and that's all it takes to get labor and other productive resources arranged according to each country's comparative advantage, America's in wheat and the Asian country's in cars.

Officially restricting American automobile imports, through an import tariff or through an outright import limit, of course, can *force* American car buyers to buy from Detroit and thus block the transfer of American resources to Kansas. Obviously, restricting imports harms the Americans who would produce cars by plowing wheat fields in Kansas. But it harms American car buyers generally, too, who wind up with fewer and therefore higher priced cars. No less badly, however, does it harm not just the Asians who would grow wheat by working automobile assembly lines but also Asian consumers generally, who have less and therefore higher priced wheat.

Bestselling Metaphors

International trade has become a field of metaphors. Titles like *Silent War* (Ira Magaziner) and *Head to Head* (Lester Thurow) help make books best-sellers. But contrary to what their authors would have us believe, the global economy really isn't a military battlefield; nor is it a basketball court. Both sides win. Nations don't compete, Friedman would say; they trade.

3

Why Prices?

The Limits of Benevolence

Hearing the name Adam Smith, most of us think immediately of his treatise *An Inquiry into the Nature and Causes of the Wealth of Nations*, published in 1776 and forever an intellectual landmark. Fewer of us, however, know of *The Theory of Moral Sentiments*, another of Adam Smith's great works, this one published in 1759. In the better known volume, *The Wealth of Nations*, Smith argues for the market, free enterprise, as the organizing principle of society. In *The Theory of Moral Sentiments*, however, and by what some people would consider sharp contrast with what he says in *The Wealth of Nations,* Smith investigates the psychological bases for acts of benevolence, and, indeed, he applauds these acts.

Do we have two Adam Smiths, then, one Adam Smith wearing a green translucent visor and elasticized armbands and the other Adam Smith carrying a *pushke*? (Yiddish: a box, usually made just of tin, but wrapped in paper announcing a charity organization's appeal.) The nineteenth-century German writers thought so and thus referred to what they called *"Das Adam Smith Problem"*.

Ronald Coase, a leading authority on Adam Smith's life and philosophy, regards *Das Adam Smith Problem* as more apparent, however, than real.[1] *The Theory of Moral Sentiments* is a book about human psychology, Coase says, and *The Wealth of Nations* a book about the organization of economic life. Yes, Adam Smith understood and greatly admired benevolence, but he understood, too, that our securing anything that resembles a comfortable standard of living requires more

---

1 Ronald H. Coase, *Essays on Economics and Economists* (Chicago: University of Chicago Press, 1995), 113-14.

11

than benevolence. We need the cooperation of people who are scattered all over the globe. We can't possibly even know their names. How can we expect their benevolence? "Man has almost constant need of help from his brethren," Adam Smith says, "and it is vain to expect it from their benevolence only." But if not from benevolence, then what does their help come from?

To this question, Adam Smith gives an answer well known to every student of economics. "It is not from the benevolence of the butcher, the brewer, or the baker that we expect our dinner," says Adam Smith in *The Wealth of Nations*, "but from their regard to their own interest. We address ourselves, not to their humanity but to their self love, and never talk to them of our necessities but of their advantages."[2]

Buffers of Civility

I think that Coase would agree to take my maternal grandfather as an example of someone who, thanks to the market economy, had the chance of addressing himself, in Adam Smith's words again, "not to their humanity but to their self love". Just a quick glance at my family photographs would leave little doubt that my grandfather was a religious Jew. Just as quick a glance at the Dearborn (Mich.) *Independent*, however, would leave equally little doubt that the newspaper's owner, the great industrialist Henry Ford, was an anti-Semite.[3] Still, for my grandfather, the religious Jew, Henry Ford, the unabashed anti-Semite, actually produced a Model-T Ford automobile. My grandfather, apparently, had *money* enough to buy the car, and for Mr. Ford, even a Jew's money was *good* enough to take in exchange for the car.

Things would likely have been very different in an authoritarian state. In an authoritarian state, Mr. Ford would have been the automobile Czar and my grandfather, the Jew, last on the automobile Czar's list of persons deserving cars. Prices are the buffers of civility. They force us, even the least tolerant of us, to behave in a civil fashion. That's a big part of my own answer to the question, "Why prices?"

---

2 Adam Smith, *The Wealth of Nations*, 26-27; quoted in Coase, 114.
3 See Neil Baldwin, *Henry Ford and the Jews: The Mass Production of Hate* (Cambridge, MA: Perseus Books Group, 2001).

...*Or When Blocked, Incivility*

I gained a fuller appreciation of how prices act as the buffer of civility by witnessing first hand, now more than thirty years ago, an example of the incivility caused by their being blocked.

Very early one morning back in 1973, during the decade's first oil crisis, I sat in a New Brunswick, New Jersey gas line, half asleep and at least a couple of hours from the pump. After a while, just to stretch my legs, I got out of my car. I happened to strike up a conversation with the driver of the car sitting behind mine.

Early each day, she had to face taking her ill daughter, at that moment sleeping in the car's back seat, to a Newark hospital. The young girl's mother, of course, would have gladly paid much more for gasoline than the nationally regulated price, roughly $.40 per gallon. She had no way, however, thanks to the price regulation, of expressing just how intensely that morning she wanted the gasoline. From the seller's point of view, her demand for gasoline seemed no stronger than mine did. We both were a long way from getting it.

Car by car, we both made our way forward, hoping that, when we got to the pumps, there would be gasoline left for us. Eventually, my turn came, and then hers. With gas in the tank, I headed for home, and she, I imagine, thankful that this time, anyway, the gasoline hadn't run out before she got some for herself, headed for the hospital.

When I got home, I did something that I don't do very often nowadays, turned on the television set. When I did, I heard a familiar jingle, advertising for one of those honeymoon resorts in eastern Pennsylvania's Pocono Mountains. I looked up at the T.V. set and saw superimposed on the ad that had been running for years and years something new, a flashing message: *"Gas, seven days a week. No lines. No waiting." "Gas, seven days a week. No lines. No waiting."*

A federal regulator had decided that X gallons of gasoline should go to the Pocono Mountains region of eastern Pennsylvania and Y gallons to the central New Jersey region. The number Y may even have been bigger than the number X. But it wasn't enough bigger than the number X, apparently, to satisfy central New Jersey's demand for gasoline, not at the legally enforced ceiling price, anyway. Had it been permitted to operate, in other words, the market would have determined a higher market-clearing price in central New Jersey than in eastern Pennsylvania.

Under ordinary circumstances, some enterprising individual, with on-the-spot knowledge of an idle tanker truck, would have transported gasoline from Pennsylvania to New Jersey. The increased supply in New Jersey and the reduced supply in Pennsylvania would have brought the two market-clearing prices into line with one another, except for the cost of transporting the gasoline. Until it was eliminated in 1981, when President Reagan took office, the price ceiling, enforced by fines and penalties, worked like a giant dam to keep the gasoline from flowing in the right direction.

Prices Work

When they're permitted to do so, prices convey information concerning real scarcities. When oil becomes scarcer than before, its higher price registers the increased scarcity and thereby encourages us to use it more carefully. We don't have to know what has caused oil's increased scarcity—a ruptured pipeline, an oil producers' cartel, a labor strike, or the beginning of the summer driving season. Whatever its cause, the increased scarcity of oil is a fact of economic life, and we have to deal with it as best we can.

But how, a listener wants to know, how can I say that, in 2003, oil has become scarcer than it was last year? Like me, he has been driving long enough to remember the gas lines of the early and late 1970s. In 2003, as he says, we see no lines.

The question has a simple enough answer, namely, that the higher price has done its job. The higher price, that is, has encouraged people to economize their use of gasoline. We need prices, then, to make known publicly the state of real scarcities. A 1970s-style attempt to regulate gasoline prices at the pump would turn gasoline's recently increased scarcity into a shortage—into the lines and inconveniences that the questioner remembers all too well.

The Price Called "Interest"

The interest rate is a price, too, but it doesn't get anywhere near full credit for the job that it does allocating the scarce resource called "capital". To more fully appreciate interest and the job that it does, it may be instructive to imagine the idealized workings of a non-market economy. With a little imagination, we can see that even a socialist utopia would need an interest rate.

At their conferences and conventions, engineers and scientists would very happily write down a long list of the projects that, if given the chance, they would undertake. "Build a bridge here", "dig a tunnel there", "put a man on Mars"—these are just a few of the proposals that we'd get. We're dealing here with people who are extremely smart, and just as imaginative, too, and their list of "wouldn't it be great if" projects would go on and on and on still further. The projects proposed would take much time to complete, and even when completed, they would provide their benefits not all at once but very, very slowly. *The Great Bridge*—the Brooklyn Bridge, that is—to mention one of the best-selling historian David McCullough's titles—opened in May 1883, thirteen and one-half years after work on that engineering marvel had begun, and more than 120 years later, it still gets New Yorkers over the East River and then back again every day.

Because they take much time to complete and because they take even longer to yield their full benefits, these engineering and scientific projects come at a cost, namely, the availability of goods to consume today; resources devoted to these investment projects can't be employed producing things for use today. In the absence of a capital market, somebody would actually have to decide which of these time intensive projects we should pursue and which of the projects we should forego. But how? What decision rule should the socialist planner use?

Suppose that the socialist planner told the scientists and engineers that his ministry would approve undertaking any project promising to repay its cost. That would be no decision rule at all, of course, because most every project would *eventually* repay its cost. Unless people wanted to have all of their resources devoted to future consumption, the planner would need a decision rule more stringent than just a project's eventually repaying its cost. The planner could say, "All right, then, we'll go ahead with any investment project that will repay its cost in no more than twenty years." And if even the socialist planner's twenty-year rule left too little for people to eat today, the planner might give the project not twenty but just ten years to repay its cost.

The socialist planner's giving the project just ten years instead of twenty to repay its cost, and then, if people *still* complained of being hungry, perhaps giving it only five years instead of ten, would be the same thing as requiring the project to pay a higher annual percentage return. The five-year limit would remove some projects from consideration and thereby release resources to satisfy more immediate and apparently more pressing wants. For the individuals who receive it, interest helps provide for the future, true. For the community as a whole, however, even a community that prohibits receiving it, interest limits the demand for capital and thus helps provide for the *present*.

A world without the price that we call "interest", then, if we could even conceive of such a thing, would be a very hungry place, indeed; we'd have a lot of waiting to do. The private capital market, in a more public and fully informed way than any socialist planner could do it, raises the bar that the engineers and the scientists have to clear before they get the signal to go ahead with their projects. And it's a good thing, too, especially for those of us who, like the woman whose daughter needed daily automobile transportation to the hospital, want things immediately or at least in the not-*too*-distant future.

4

From the Man of Steel.... A Story of Interest

"It's a Bird! It's a Plane! It's...."

Most everyone who grew up during the 1950s knows what, or actually who, *it* is. "Yes", the weekly television show's prologue continued, "it's Superman—strange visitor from another planet who came to earth with powers and abilities far beyond those of mortal men. Faster than a speeding bullet, more powerful than a locomotive, able to leap tall buildings in a single bound. Superman—who can change the course of mighty rivers, bend steel in his bare hands, and who, disguised as Clark Kent, mild mannered reporter for a great metropolitan newspaper, fights the never ending battle for truth, justice, and the American way."

Well, the American way is capitalism, and like motherhood and apple pie, the price that we call "interest" is as American as it gets. Perhaps through one of Superman's adventures, we can learn something about what determines that price.

Professor Periwinkle

I'd wait eagerly each week to see Kent, who, when the call for Superman went out, would step into a telephone booth and by removing his suit to reveal the caped uniform beneath—the inscribed letter "S" on his chest—transform himself into the man of steel; Perry White, the irascible editor of the *Daily Planet*; Jimmy Olsen, the *Planet's* trouble-prone cub reporter; and Lois Lane, Olsen's more experienced partner, who suspects but doesn't want to admit that Superman is really the *Planet's* own and far less heroic Clark Kent.

My favorite, however, though he didn't make an appearance in every week's show, was Superman's offbeat friend, the inventor Professor Periwinkle. Periwinkle's inventions never work—they never work, that is, until the show in which he comes up with a machine emitting beams that will double anything left in his laboratory for a year, anything, that is, except money.

The kindly soul that he is, Professor Periwinkle makes the machine available to anyone in Metropolis who wants to use it. The first chances go to Jimmy Olsen and Lois Lane. "Would you like to have another coat?" Periwinkle proudly asks young Jimmy. "Just hang your coat right here, Jimmy, and a year from now you'll have two coats." "And Lois!" he continues excitedly. "You'd like another bracelet, wouldn't you? Yes, yes…of course you would! Just leave yours right here on my desk."

Before long, however, the good professor's machine falls into the wrong hands. The underworld of Metropolis has somehow gotten hold of some Kryptonite, the only element (it comes from Superman's childhood home, the now defunct planet Krypton) that can weaken the man of steel, but not enough of it to do him any permanent damage. Periwinkle's machine, one of them realizes while reading about it in that day's *Planet*, is their answer. In a year's time, one grain of kryptonite will become two grains; in another year's time, the two grains will become four grains…. Their grain of Kryptonite will eventually grow into an overpowering amount of the glowing green stuff deadly to Superman. To finally be rid of Superman, all his enemies need is Periwinkle's machine and a little bit of patience. Sweet talking their way past Periwinkle, the criminals get into his laboratory, tie him up along with his two friends, and then, taking the captives and the machine, make a clean getaway. Once back at their hideout, they waste no time at all setting the stolen machine to work on the kryptonite.

Well, you know how these 1950s shows work out. Superman, whose X-ray vision puts him on to what the bad guys are up to, foils their plans. He collars the criminals and, of course, rescues Jimmy, Lois, and Periwinkle. Then, wanting his machine never to fall into the wrong hands again, Periwinkle has Superman launch it permanently into outer space. After Superman flies off, Clark Kent, awkwardly straightening his necktie and adjusting his windowpane eyeglasses, reappears to face Lois Lane's uncomfortable questions concerning his whereabouts the past several hours. "Where have *you* been Clark?" she wants to know, noticing yet again that Kent and Superman bear an amazingly strong resemblance to one another.

Of Interest

In this story's introduction, I promised not just an interesting story but also a story of interest. What *of* interest, then, in the bustling city of Metropolis?

Provided that his machine doubles the laboratory's contents in one year, no matter how fully Periwinkle packs the room, and provided, of course, that he gives everyone a chance to benefit from his machine, the interest rate has to be 100 percent. Just think of what you could do if the interest rate were any lower than 100 percent. You could buy a car with money borrowed at, say, 10 percent and then leave the car with Periwinkle. A year later, you'd come back to find two cars. You'd sell one of the cars, repay the loan, and pocket the 90 percent profit. Then, you'd start all over again. The opportunity would be so obvious that everyone would want to get in on the deal; everybody would want to borrow. The increased demand for loans would take the interest rate up toward 100 percent. Only when the interest rate reached 100 percent would the door close on this get-rich-quick scheme.

As it turns out, however, Periwinkle's machine fails the important assumption that it will double the laboratory's contents in one year no matter how fully packed the laboratory may be. The more fully Periwinkle packs his laboratory, the longer the machine takes to work its reproductive magic; and Periwinkle has already packed so much of the reporters' stuff into his laboratory that the gauge showing how many years the machine will take to double the room's contents reads not "1", as it did earlier, but "4".

Jimmy Olsen, too, in effect, anyway, has a gauge, and so does Lois Lane. Their gauges show how many years the two reporters are willing to wait while the machine doubles what they've left in Periwinkle's lab. The more stuff that Jimmy and Lois leave in Periwinkle's lab, the more quickly they expect his machine to work—and already the readings on the reporters' gauges have *fallen* from "10" to "4".

If the reporters left any more stuff with Periwinkle, the reading on his machine's gauge would rise to "5" and the readings on their own gauges would fall to "3": the machine would take five years to double the lab's contents, and Jimmy and Lois would be willing to wait no more than three years. Together, then, now that all three gauges read "4", Jimmy and Lois give Periwinkle the nod that he has been waiting for. He throws the switch, and their four-year wait begins. During each of those years, the lab's contents will grow by 25 percent. Meanwhile, to reflect the economic fundamentals that economists summarize by using the phrase "productivity and thrift"—"productivity", the ability that Periwinkle's machine gives Jimmy and Lois to transform present goods into an even greater quantity of future goods; "thrift", the reporters' willingness to do without present goods while they wait for the greater quantity of future goods—the interest rate in Metropolis settles at 25 percent.

Enter Mr. Greenspan?

Though certainly not the whole story of interest—interest comes up again, in Chapter 5, where we'll see it as something deeply embedded in the economy, showing up not just as the price of loans but also in how expensive various goods are relative to one another—this chapter's little story may still serve a very good purpose. It casts doubt on depicting Alan Greenspan as himself deciding what the interest rate should be and then, somehow, just making it so. Mr. Greenspan is a very savvy fellow, true. But he's no Periwinkle. Nor does he have coats and cars just to give people who want a piece of Periwinkle-type magic. Mr. Greenspan does have as much money as he cares to print, of course, but money isn't, at bottom, the real story of interest.

5

Microeconomics Writ Large

What is Microeconomics?

As the prefix "micro" in the word "microeconomics" suggests, we economists care about the economy's small parts—consumers and firms, to take two obvious examples. We care about them, yes, but not necessarily for their own sake. We're not marketers, nor are we production managers. Then why *do* we care about consumers? Why do we care about *firms?* We care about the small parts of the economy because, for one thing, we want to know what larger picture would emerge if they came together, cohesively, as the schematic diagram that we call "economic theory" says that they should. In this sense and contrary to the impression that I'm afraid far too many economics majors leave school with, microeconomics is no less about the economy *as a whole* than is macroeconomics. Hence this story's title, "Microeconomics Writ Large".

A System of Interlocking Parts

I want to encourage thinking of the economy, then, as a unified system of interlocking parts. An example will help explain what I mean by "unified system" and by "interlocking parts". The example, I confess, doesn't make for anything like a just-sit-back-and-listen story. Have a pencil and a piece of paper handy; you'll want to check my arithmetic.

To get underway, we'll need two production recipes. Producing one cake, let's say, requires (in addition to ingredients that we have in superabundant quantities) two eggs and one cup of sugar. Producing one dozen cookies, however, requires one egg and two cups of sugar. The cake is the egg-intensive good; producing a cake requires more eggs per cup of sugar than producing the dozen cookies does. The dozen cookies, on the other hand, are the sugar-intensive good; producing a dozen cookies requires more sugar per egg than producing a cake does.

We won't worry about where the eggs and the sugar come from. Every month, five eggs and four cups of sugar just appear, like manna from heaven. People rush out to scoop the stuff up and then sell it. For now, we'll attach to each egg a $1 price tag and to each cup of sugar a $2 price tag. It's just a matter of arithmetic, then, to calculate the price of a cake and the price of a dozen cookies. A cake sells for $4 ($1 per egg x 2 eggs + $2 per cup of sugar x 1 cup of sugar), and the dozen cookies sell for $5 (I leave the arithmetic to you).

Now let's put the all-important question to our consumers. At these prices, $4 per cake and $5 per dozen cookies, we ask them, how many cakes do you want per month, and how many dozen cookies? They want two cakes per month and one dozen cookies; that's their answer. Giving consumers these demanded quantities requires using 5 eggs (4 eggs to produce the cakes and 1 more egg to produce the cookies) and 4 cups of sugar (again, I leave the arithmetic to you). The derived monthly demands for eggs and for sugar are exactly the quantities that fall earthward each month. These two prices, then, $1 per egg and $2 per cup of sugar, and the implied prices of the consumers' goods, $4 per cake and $5 per dozen cookies, are equilibrium prices. At these prices, all four markets clear. For eggs, for sugar, for cake, and for cookies, that is, supply equals demand. By checking to make sure that all four markets clear simultaneously, we've taken a first step toward looking at the economy as "a unified system of interlocking parts".

Sometimes, thinking of the economy as a system whose parts should fit together leads to surprising conclusions. Take, for example, as seemingly simple a question as what would happen if the monthly manna deliveries increased, say by three eggs? The egg, of course, would become cheaper. So would the cake, whose production, remember, is egg intensive. By no means, however, would that be the end of the story.

At the lower price per cake, consumers would demand a larger monthly quantity of cakes. To produce more cakes, however, the cake bakers would require not just more eggs but more sugar, too, sugar that would have to come from the cookie bakers. Cutting back monthly cookie production by one dozen would release 1 egg and 2 cups of sugar, the very quantities that the cake bakers, who use a 2:1 egg-to-sugar ratio, would need to employ the 3 new eggs. But would the cookie bakers cut back their monthly production? They would indeed cut back production, and for good reason: the increased demand for sugar would raise the price per cup of sugar; because the dozen cookies are the sugar intensive good, the higher price per cup of sugar would reflect itself in a higher price per dozen cookies; and at the higher price per dozen cookies, consumers would want a smaller monthly quantity of cookies. More eggs appear each month, then, but the result wouldn't be just cheaper eggs, together with more and therefore cheaper cakes. In an economic system whose parts fit together, more eggs each month would mean more expensive sugar, too, and together with more expensive sugar, fewer and therefore more expensive cookies.

So Far, Everything's Relative

Here, the term "more expensive" means more expensive relative to other things, cookies relative to cake and sugar relative to eggs; that's all the term "more expensive" means. Strangely, or so it would surely seem to us, people in our story wouldn't care at all about the general level of dollar prices. They'd have no reason to care about the general level of dollar prices. Say, for example, that, somehow, each baking ingredient's equilibrium dollar price just doubled, the price per egg becoming $2 and the price per cup of sugar $4. The consumers' goods, of course, would become twice as expensive, too, $8 per cake and $10 per dozen cookies. No one would care about the doubled prices of consumers' goods, however, because every month people would earn twice as much income as they did before for collecting and then selling the very same quantity of heaven sent eggs and sugar.

Because no one would care about the dollar price level, its changing wouldn't alter anybody's market behavior; no corrective behavior would ensue to reverse the postulated doubling of dollar prices and restore them to their former heights. The system's dollar prices could double, triple, or even quadruple themselves, and the change wouldn't make any difference at all, to anyone. Indeterminate, adrift, the general *level* of dollar prices could be anything, it seems, provided that the individual dollar prices stood in the correct relation to one another: the price of an egg at one-half the price of a cup of sugar and the price of a cake at eighty percent the price of a dozen cookies. To make the dollar price level (and not just the relative prices, 1:2 and 0.8:1) determinate—stable—something has to make people *care* about it. And, obviously, to judge by our seeing that the price level doesn't just jump about, something does make people care about it.

Caring about the Price Level

The something that makes people care about the general price level is money. In the story as we've told it thus far, money has had no actual concrete existence. Oh sure, we've used the word "dollar". But until now, "dollar" has been just an abstract accounting unit, a unit used for expressing prices. The real world dollar, however, is more than just an abstract accounting unit. Besides being an abstract accounting unit, the dollar is something concrete, an actual medium of exchange.

A world with no medium of exchange—a world, that is, of no transactions other than purely barter transactions—is hard to imagine and probably has never existed. In a world of purely barter transactions, making a sale would mean finding someone who wanted to buy exactly what you had to sell and also wanted to sell exactly what you wanted to buy. The costs of finding such a person, your own personal mirror image, so to speak, and finding such a person for each and every transaction, furthermore, would be truly exorbitant.

Having a routinely used medium of exchange—for us, it's predominantly the Federal Reserve note—eliminates these transactions costs, and people find it convenient to maintain adequate reserves of it. "Adequate reserves", of course, means adequate as judged in terms of their purchasing power. Our consumers' answer to the question, then, "How many cakes do you want per month, and how many dozen cookies?" depends not just on one good's dollar price *relative* to the other good's dollar price but also on an index of the dollar prices themselves. A higher general level of dollar prices would make people's money holdings smaller in purchasing-power terms and thus would weaken the demand both for cake and for cookies. Money and having whatever they consider adequate holdings of it is what makes people care about the dollar price level and thus what makes their market behavior depend on it and not just on relative prices.

General Equilibrium

A money balance is just one of the several things that consumers find it desirable to have. A consumer's decisions concerning quantities demanded of money, of cake, and of cookies aren't made independently, however, one decision, then another, and then the third. Decisions concerning quantities demanded are of necessity interlocking decisions. The consumer, who buys some cookies and some cakes and who, just to be on the safe side, wants to hold in reserve some quantity of the medium of exchange, makes these decisions together, as part of a coherent single plan based on market prices, both relative prices and dollar prices. But where do these market prices come from in the first place? To the individual consumer, the answer to this question can't be at all obvious. Market prices emerge from the workings of the economic system as a whole, and the economic system as a whole lies outside the individual consumer's field of vision.

The individual consumer's being unable to see the economic system as a whole, however, shouldn't keep us from understanding the basic logic of the system. Let's just suppose that for each different combination of cake's relative price and the community's money holdings relative to either dollar prices or, as I'll tell the story here, dollar *incomes*, we knew how many cakes and how many dozen cookies consumers wanted to buy. With this information, we could find the particular combination of relative price and income-measured money holdings at which consumers demand cakes and cookies in the quantities whose monthly production just exhaust the monthly supplies of eggs and sugar. Let's assume that this particular combination is 0.8 dozen cookies per cake (or, equivalently, 2 eggs per cup of sugar) as before, but together now with money holdings equivalent to three months' (.25 year's) income. No other combination would permit markets to clear. A higher than 0.8 cookie-price of cake would tilt consumers' demand toward cookies, the sugar intensive good, creating an excess demand for sugar and an excess supply of eggs. Consumers' having money balances equivalent to something less than three months' income, on the other hand, would weaken demand for both goods and thus create an excess supply of both ingredients. When the price of a cake is 0.8 dozen cookies and they have *monetary* reserves equal to .25 year's income, however, consumers want 2 cakes and 1 dozen cookies each month; and producing these quantities each month requires using the available five eggs and four cups of sugar.

These two numbers, then, 0.8 and .25, are the system's equilibrium real values. Each number expresses one thing's value in terms of another thing: 0.8 expresses the cake's value in terms of cookies, and .25 expresses the dollar quantity of money as a fraction of the system's annual income flow. As if it were a self-solving system of two simultaneous equations— one equation requiring the fixed monthly supply of eggs to equal the derived monthly demand for eggs and the other equation requiring the same thing for sugar—the economic system of markets ferrets out its equilibrium real values.

Dropping the Nominal Anchor

It's the government's business to translate the system's equilibrium real values into their corresponding nominal, or dollar, values. By setting the dollar quantity of money, the government can make the system's dollar values as high or as low as it cares to make them. Again, our system's equilibrium real values are 0.8 dozen cookies per cake and a quantity of money equivalent to .25 year's income. To translate these equilibrium real values into the particular set of nominal values that we started this general equilibrium story with—$4 per cake, $5 per dozen cookies, $1 per egg, and $2 per cup of sugar—the government would have to set the quantity of money at exactly $39. And we'll assume that the government does so set it, even if, as we explain why the required quantity of money is $39, we have Mr. Greenspan, who manages the country's money supply, just fling the paper bills from Marine Corps One, the president's helicopter.

The low flying helicopter's door opens, then, and out go the paper bills totaling $39. The public has no choice but to hold the entire $39 money supply; after the drop and the ensuing scramble to pick up the money, every paper bill has to be in *somebody's* pocket. The dollar quantity of money is $39, therefore, because that's what the airborne Mr. Greenspan chooses to make it. On the ground, however, the economic system has determined that the dollar quantity of money should be the equivalent of .25 year's income. Though always in somebody's possession, then, each paper dollar changes hands 4 times per year, converting the Greenspan-set $39 stock of money into the required $156 annual *flow* of spending and hence income. The $156 annual flow of income is the first of our general equilibrium system's nominal values.

Together with the annual flow of income come the system's dollar prices. We know that, each year, people spend $156. They buy 12 dozen cookies, and they buy cakes, 24 of them, worth another 19.2 [(0.8) 24=19.2] dozen cookies—a total, in effect, of 31.2 dozen cookies. A dozen cookies, therefore, must go for $5 ($156/31.2=$5), and a cake for $4 [(0.8) $5=$4]. The prices of the consumers' goods are, indeed, just what we said they would be if the government set the dollar quantity of money at $39.

So, too, as just a little bit more arithmetic will show, are the prices of the ingredients just what we said they'd be if the government set the dollar quantity of money at the $39 total. The economic system determines that the cake has 0.8 of the dozen cookies' value. The ingredients that the cake recipe calls for, therefore, must have the same total value as 0.8 of the ingredients that the cookies recipe calls for: 2 eggs plus 1 cup of sugar must have the same total value, in other words, as 0.8 egg plus 1.6 cups of sugar [0.8(1 egg + 2 cups of sugar)]. This equality of composite values gives 1 egg the value of one-half cup of sugar. The cake, then, which costs $4, calls for using 2 eggs, but together with sugar worth another 2 eggs. Each egg must be worth $1, therefore, and because the economic system determines an egg to be half as valuable as a cup of sugar, each cup of sugar worth $2.

From the ingredients' prices, incomes and their distribution follow. Each year, by selling their 60 eggs–48 eggs to the cake bakers and 12 to the cookie bakers—the egg merchants earn $60. And by selling their 48 cups of sugar each year—24 cups to the cake bakers and 24 to the cookie bakers—the sugar merchants earn $96 per year. Nominal incomes total $156 per year, just as we knew they would have to; the $156 that consumers spend each year on cakes and cookies is also the $156 income that they earn each year by selling their eggs and sugar.

These figures, then, anchored by the government-set $39 quantity of money, are the system's nominal values: $156 income per year; $5 per dozen cookies; $4 per cake; $2 per cup of sugar; and $1 per egg. With these values established, people make market decisions that enable the economic system as a whole to work. If the government doubled the dollar quantity of money, making it a $78 instead of $39 total, then the system's nominal values would double, too. Nominal income would rise to $312 per year, and the list of dollar prices would read: $10 per dozen cookies, $8 per cake; $4 per cup of sugar; and $2 per egg. The system's equilibrium real values, however, wouldn't change. A cake would still be worth 0.8 dozen cookies, an egg worth one-half cup of sugar, and the (now doubled) dollar quantity of money worth .25 year's income.

Waiting for Value

I've neglected thus far to mention something peculiar about the cookies, actually about the package that the dozen cookies come in. Each month, the standard, one-dozen package dispenses just six of its twelve cookies. Only after a month has elapsed do the remaining six cookies become ready to eat. Cookies can't be purchased, not even singly, furthermore, except from a one-dozen package.

Our actually consuming twelve cookies each month, then, means that over the month somebody has to hold two half-empty packages of cookies. Somebody, that is, has to wait. Somebody, even if that "somebody" is just the baker of cookies, who until now has been involved not as an earner of income but as a mere hobbyist, has to keep value—value in the form of twelve not-yet-ready-to-eat cookies *on their way* to becoming edible—tied up through time, instead of selling them and using the proceeds to finance current consumption. (I use "ready-to-eat cookies" as a metaphor for things like "housing" and "transportation", services delivered over time, piecemeal, by durable assets such as residential buildings and automobiles, which, like the story's standard packages of cookies, someone must hold and maintain.) "It is this waiting," said Sir Hubert Henderson, on whose Cambridge Economic Handbooks classic, *Supply and Demand*, generations of English economists cut their teeth, "that is the essential reality underlying the phenomena of capital and interest" (p. 98).

Every bit as much as it requires eggs and sugar, producing "ready-to-eat cookies" requires yet a third ingredient, "waiting for value through time". Eggs and sugar aren't available in unlimited quantities, of course, and neither is waiting for value. Owing to its scarcity, the ingredient that we call "waiting for value", like eggs and sugar, has a price; and just as it has to cover the price of eggs and the price of sugar, the price of a ready-to-eat cookie, if the cookie is to be produced at all, has to cover the price of waiting, too. The price of waiting for value is interest, and its existence in this somewhat caloric general equilibrium story means that consumers have to pay more for twelve ready-to-eat cookies than they have to pay for a standard one-dozen package of cookies.

To many of us, the connection between interest and the price of ready-to-eat cookies will be something altogether new. Interest is more familiar to most people, of course, as the price of a money loan. But the price of a money loan is just one form in which the even more fundamental price, the price of the ingredient "waiting for value", expresses itself. The premium that the story's twelve ready-to-eat cookies command over the standard package of one dozen cookies is another expression of that even more fundamental price. Arbitrage, taking advantage of cross-market price discrepancies, tends to keep the two expressions of the price paid for the ingredient that we call "waiting for value" equal to each other.

To show how arbitrage would work to keep the two expressions of waiting's price equal to one another, let's assume that such a cross-market price discrepancy existed. Say, for example, that 12 ready-to-eat cookies commanded a 10 percent premium over the standard package of 12 cookies but that you could get a month's money loan for 5 percent. I'm sure that under these circumstances you would know exactly what to do. You would borrow enough money to buy two standard one-dozen packages of cookies, half of whose combined contents, the 12 ready-to-eat cookies, you would sell immediately. You would wait a month while the remaining 12 cookies became ready to eat, and then you would sell them. Then, you would pay off the lender and put in your own pocket as pure profit the difference between what you got for the cookies and what you paid the lender.

Seeing this get-rich-quick opportunity, people would start lining up to get loans, and the increase in the demand for loans would push up the interest charged on them. The increased supply of ready-to-eat cookies, however, together with the increased demand for standard, one-dozen packages of cookies, would push down the price premium on ready-to-eat cookies. The two manifestations of interest, the loan rate and the premium that 12 ready-to-eat cookies carry over a standard package of 12 cookies, would come into equality, then, at some value between 5 percent and 10 percent—let's say 8 percent per month—the rate required to bring the demand for waiting into equality with total available quantity of it. Actually, arbitrage would act quickly enough and powerfully enough to prevent the postulated cross-market price discrepancy from arising in the first place.

Asking the Right Questions

Jointly with the economic system's other real values, the interest rate (for reasons that I hope the preceding section has made sufficiently clear, some economists call it "the normal rate of profit") has a numerical value determined by the system itself. It is a meaningless question, then, though a question we often hear, even from people who should know that it's meaningless, to ask how the general economy would react to a change in the interest rate. No price *just changes*, altogether on its own. It changes—not alone, but together with other prices, the quantities of cake and cookies produced, and how the fixed monthly supplies of eggs and sugar get allocated to producing cake and producing cookies—if and when something whose value is set outside the economic system, some basic fact of nature, changes.

Some of these basic facts of nature are purely technical. The technical facts of nature include the system's monthly endowment of eggs and sugar, for example, and also the rate at which the cookie package dispenses its contents. Other facts of nature, however, are non-technical. The non-technical facts of nature include the state of consumers' preferences, not just their preferences concerning what to *do* now, eat or hold durable assets, either money balances or not-yet-ready-to-eat cookies, but also their preferences concerning *what* to eat now, cakes or cookies. A properly formulated question would ask how the system's equilibrium real values, the interest rate among them, would change if one of these basic facts of nature, technical or non-technical, happened to change.

We've already considered a change in one of nature's technical facts, the monthly endowment of eggs. Let's imagine now, then, that one of the non-technical facts of nature changes. Consumers' basic preferences shift, let's say, away from cake and toward ready-to-eat cookies. The shift of consumers' basic preferences away from cake and toward ready-to-eat cookies would weaken the derived demand for eggs, of course, because eggs figure intensively in producing cake. The price per egg would drop, then, as would the price per cake. The derived demand for both sugar and waiting, on the other hand, would become stronger, because both sugar and waiting figure intensively in producing ready-to-eat cookies. Both the price of sugar and the price of waiting would rise, then, as would the price of the ready-to-eat cookie.

The higher price of waiting—the higher interest rate—might actually have a doubled-barreled effect on the ready-to-eat cookie's price. "Waiting" means waiting for value, and the demand shift in favor of ready-to-eat cookies could very well raise not just the price of waiting but also the value amount of waiting tied up in production as unfinished cookies. The value amount of waiting required to *produce* each ready-to-eat cookie could increase, in other words, making the ready-to-eat cookies even more waiting (i.e., capital) intensive than they were before consumers' preferences happened to shift toward them.

Together with the higher price of waiting and the higher price of sugar, the increased value amount of waiting required to produce each ready-to-eat cookie would work to increase its price. The higher price would to some degree dampen consumers' assumed newfound enthusiasm for ready-to-eat cookies, keeping the derived demand for waiting and the derived demand for sugar from outstripping the fixed monthly supplies of those two ingredients. A lower price per cake, on the other hand, would to some degree rekindle consumers' assumed weakened interest in cake and thus keep the derived demand for eggs strong enough to exhaust the fixed monthly supply of eggs. At these changed prices, changed quantities of cakes and cookies, and changed cake-versus-cookie allocations of eggs and sugar, general economic equilibrium would re-establish itself. Once again, markets would clear.

Macroeconomics Previewed

This sketch, then, is our cookies-and-cake and eggs-and-sugar economy as it would take shape in a frictionless world, the world of general equilibrium microeconomics. Simultaneously, on each of the system's markets, supply equals demand. Because all markets clear simultaneously, nobody winds up disappointed. Sellers of eggs find buyers, that is, and buyers of sugar find vendors. Sellers of cakes find customers, and, to their delight, cookie lovers find Mrs. Fields. Some of that lady's otherwise more impulsive customers even come to regard patience as warranted. A month, they find, isn't all that long a wait for one of her delicious confections. The individual pieces fit together just as they should, to form a larger, cohesive picture of the economy as a whole. The larger, cohesive picture, again, as my title says, is "Microeconomics Writ Large".

Sometimes, however, although the pieces of the general economic equilibrium puzzle fit together, some obstruction blocks their actually coming together to form that larger, cohesive picture. The larger, cohesive picture that we expect to see fails to take shape. The obstruction and its disruptive effects form the subject matter of macroeconomics. In this chapter, the section entitled "*Caring about the Price Level*" may already have done something to show what the most likely obstruction is, and in the next chapter, the section entitled "*A Honeymooners' Story*" will, I hope, do still a bit more.

6

Who Says That Money Is No Joke.... A Honeymooners' Story

No Funny Money

The appearance just recently of the blue, green, and yellow, supposedly harder-to-counterfeit paper money reminded me of an incident that I witnessed some years ago. It took place at the local supermarket.

There I stood that Sunday afternoon, not quite minding my own business, next in line to pay for groceries. The customer ahead of me, who to pay his bill had used his debit card, wanted cash back. The cashier handed the man his register tape, together with the cash that he had asked for. The customer examined the paper bills very closely, and then, trying to conceal his anxiety with humor, said, "Don't give me any of this funny money. I want the real stuff." By "funny money", the customer meant the then new twenty-dollar bill, the first Federal Reserve note to display an enlarged portrait, Andrew Jackson's. The cashier seemed to understand, and with a quiet chuckle, did as the man asked.

I have to confess that the new twenty-dollar bill looked pretty strange to me, too—like what my fellow shopper called "funny money". In a very important sense, however, *all* money is funny money, and once we get the joke, we can more clearly see what really makes money matter and why a shortage of it can cause serious problems. "Money," the Austrian born economist Joseph Schumpeter wrote in 1930, "is nothing but a technical aid for effecting transactions—a game chip without significance itself."[1] A story that back in the late 1950s, TV's

---

1 Quoted in Parth J. Shah and Leland B. Yeager, "Schumpeter on Monetary Determinacy", *History of Political Economy*, 1994, Fall, 443-64.

golden era, might well have cast Jackie Gleason's bus driver Ralph Kramden and his *Honeymooners'* sidekick, Art Carney's sewer worker Ed Norton, will help us understand what Schumpeter meant by "game chip" and "without significance itself".

A Honeymooners' Story

Loyal Raccoons both, Ralph and Ed have already checked into the hotel that has the great misfortune this year of hosting that organization's annual convention. While Ed readies their paraphernalia for the first night's hi-jinx—water balloons, hand buzzers, and all the rest of the stuff that they've collected since last year's convention—Ralph wanders down to the hotel's lobby and, there, asks the desk clerk to hold a $100 bill overnight. The desk clerk, whom I'll call person A, takes the $100 bill and puts it in the hotel's big safe. As he swings the safe's heavy door shut, however, he begins to think. He owes person B $100, and the payment is due tonight. His own debtor, person Z, has promised, however, that bright and early tomorrow morning, he'll appear with the $100 that he owes the clerk. "Can I get away with this?" the desk clerk wonders, glancing furtively about, as if worried that somebody might actually have heard his incriminating thoughts.

He has no choice but to try. He knows that he won't find his creditor, B, the corner capitalist, in any mood to negotiate another extension of his long overdue $100 loan. As soon as Kramden disappears behind the closed elevator doors, then, the desk clerk takes the $100 bill from the safe, goes through the hotel's revolving door, and crosses a street very busy with automobile traffic. Finding B at his usual post on the opposite corner, the desk clerk, trying hard to look inconspicuous, very nervously hands him the bill. Having made good the debt to his creditor, the desk clerk heads back to the hotel quickly, hoping and praying that Z will actually show up the next morning.

Despite the threatening scowl on his face, B is actually much relieved to have the $100 bill in his hand. He uses it to repay person C, who then, to make good a debt of his own, passes it along to D. All down the line the bill goes, from D to E and then to F, making its way, finally, to Z, who, as promised, appears early the next morning to pay the hotel clerk.

Much to the clerk's relief, Z hands him a $100 bill, but not a moment too soon; for just as the clerk gets the bill back into the safe, the freshly polished elevator doors open wide and out struts Kramden, in full-dress Raccoon regalia. "Yes sir, right away Mr. Kramden, sir," says the desk clerk, and a bit too obligingly the bellhop within earshot can't help thinking. "I'll get the bill out of the safe for you right away." He has some trouble opening the safe, but finally does. He takes out the $100 bill and hands it to Kramden, expecting him to put it safely in his wallet and depart the hotel lobby. As the desk clerk's jaw drops, however, Kramden pulls aside the tail of his coonskin cap (at the lodge's annual convention, every loyal Raccoon wears his coonskin cap backwards and greets fellow raccoons by shaking the cap's tail) and uses the $100 bill to light a very large cigar. "It's funny money. Got it yesterday at the gag store downtown," Ralph announces proudly, while holding the bill's remains aloft, still ablaze. "Just wanted to see whether you'd go for it."

Funny money, yes. But, today, from A to Z, it's been business as usual. Money is important, as I hope this little (and, one reader wants me to admit, more than a little fanciful) story shows, not nearly so much for what it is as for what it does.

7

Macroeconomics, or Diagnosis:
Money

System-Wide Failure

Even during an economic depression, when they're unemployed, workers still want to feed, clothe, and shelter themselves and their families. No less strongly than the unemployed laborers want to resume working, however, do the closed down employers want to reopen their plants. On the one hand, then, the unemployed workers would become customers if they had jobs, and on the other hand, the closed down employers would begin hiring again if they had customers. The pieces of the depressed economy seem to fit together as they should. Nevertheless, they stubbornly resist *coming* together. People don't have jobs, after all; and the plants are closed down. We have a system-wide problem; that's all too obvious. But what is its cause?

There wouldn't be a problem (or not this particular problem, anyway) if U.S. Steel, for example, paid its workers wages as sheet metal and the supermarkets accepted sheet metal as payment for groceries. But goods and services don't exchange for other goods and services directly, labor services for sheet metal and then sheet metal for groceries. Goods and services exchange for other goods and services indirectly, through the intermediary of the distinctive asset money. What could the cause of the system-wide failure be, then, if not a shortage of money itself?

A mechanical metaphor, though it may seem simple minded, is actually very instructive. You would know exactly what to expect if you found your car standing in a pool of oil. The car isn't going to run, not for very long, anyway. No matter how well manufactured the motor's moving parts may be, to function in a coordinated way, they require adequate lubrication. Adequate lubrication for your car's motor means five quarts of Pennzoil.

Well, even during an economic depression, people want to do what they've always done. The unemployed worker, the shut-down producer—everyone would prefer to have things as they were. The economy's moving parts, in other words, are basically still intact. Without adequate *monetary* lubrication, however, the parts seize: people can't do what they want and still know how to do. But what does "adequate" mean? Adequate monetary lubrication means a quantity of money that satisfies people's demand for holdings of the monetary lubricant. Money defines the term "liquidity", and people have at least some rough idea of how much money they should hold. Five quarts of Pennzoil would cease being adequate if your motor's oil pump began to fail—if instead of lubricating the motor's moving parts, the oil began to just sit in the pan. So, too, an otherwise adequate quantity of money (defined not just as pocket cash but also deposits transferable directly, either by check or electronically) would cease being adequate if people wanted holdings of money larger than they actually had.

The Monetary Interpretation of Economic Depression

If, after having fallen, your money balance shows no evidence of returning to the level that you deem adequate, how do you go about replenishing it? It's easy enough to do—you simply exercise restraint in spending. You deposit your paycheck as usual and then simply curtail your own writing of checks. Within the constraints that your wealth poses, then, you can hold as much money as you care to hold. So can I, and so can everyone else. Here, however, as they often do in social systems, individual and overall points of view diverge. As individuals, we can each hold as much money as we care to hold, but as a community, we can't hold any more money than actually exists. When someone deposits a check, the banks just move money out of one person's account and into another person's. Our individually attempting to hold money balances that add up to more money than actually exists, then, does nothing to enlarge the aggregate of those money balances. Instead, flows of spending and income through those money balances shrink. Flows of spending and income shrink until, to the holders of money, the shrunken flows no longer look too big *relative* to the unchanged total quantity of money balances.

Now, as a matter of sheer arithmetic, a shrunken flow of spending and income has to mean either a reduced number of commercial transactions or a reduced level of prices at which those transactions take place. The chances that the required shrinkage of spending and income will occur through reduced prices alone and not at all through a reduced number of transactions, however, aren't very promising. For very good and understandable reasons, people tend to hold out for what they've come to regard as customary prices and wages.

A who-goes-first problem exists, and that problem makes it hard to get the wage-and-price level down. No one wants to go first. Sure, I would accept a lower wage—if the supermarket where I do my grocery shopping cut its prices. The supermarket would accept lower prices—if its employees cut their wage demands. People setting prices or negotiating wages don't act as if they have no idea what other people are doing; they keep one eye on what they're doing themselves and the other eye on what their fellow price setters and wage negotiators are doing. Each person has good reason to hold off on making a downward price or wage adjustment. Better to wait. Better to get a reading on what other people are going to do about their price and wage demands before reducing your own.

Eventually, however, perhaps when it begins worrying about its perishable goods, the supermarket, for example, will have to cut its prices. When the supermarket cuts its prices, other people will find it easier and even more necessary to follow suit. Meantime, however, prices remain stuck too high, and because transactions are voluntary, the shorter side— the demand side—of each market prevails. The volume of transactions in goods and services falls off; excess supplies of goods and labor persist. People have trouble earning incomes, and with their incomes reduced, people feel unable to *afford* holding money balances any larger than those they already have. Unemployment chokes off what at full employment would have been an excess demand for money holdings.

An excess demand for money causes the kind of widespread trouble that no other excess demand can cause. People who want more of some ordinary thing, say, cars, actually have to *do* something. The strengthened demand for cars registers on a specific market, and on that specific market, changes in price and in quantities supplied and demanded work to eliminate the excess demand. If government regulations block these price-andquantity adjustments, then waiting lines will form. Discouraged, some people might even decide to buy something else instead. As long as their frustrated demand turns to something other than the medium of exchange itself, the exchange of goods and services against other goods and services can continue unimpeded.

When the thing that people want more of is money, however, exchanges of goods and services against other goods and services will likely suffer, as will the production of those things. To hold more money, people don't actually have to do anything; they need only passively refrain from spending it. Money, in other words, unlike ordinary things, lacks a market (and a price) of its own, a "money market" that would work to bring the supply of and the demand for money more or less automatically into line with one another again and by so doing keep the system of production and exchange going.

Sufficiently lower prices and wages would eliminate the excess demand for money holdings, of course, but getting an across-the-board fall in prices and wages takes time because no one has much incentive to go first. The apparent cure, lower prices and wages, can be every bit as bad, furthermore, as the disease itself. For one thing, once prices and wages do eventually begin falling, people may expect them to continue falling. People may therefore postpone buying things, expecting to get them at even lower prices later. The economy's oil pump, to go back to the mechanical metaphor, might begin to fail, that is, and the system's reduced "monetary pressure" would make an even larger drop in wages and prices necessary.

For another thing, as prices fall, people will find their debts—home and car payments, for example, because they're fixed in dollar terms— harder to shoulder. Debtors will be expected to repay dollars that buy more than they bought when the repayment schedule was written. Some people who before the deflation were financially quite solvent will therefore find themselves staring at bankruptcy, and like the common cold, bankruptcy is catchy. It's a catch-22, then, to use the title of Joseph Heller's popular 1960s novel: we'll have problems if prices and wages don't fall, and we'll have problems if they do.

An excess demand for money is not only more painful to cure than an excess demand for any ordinary thing but also more difficult for people even to diagnose correctly. No one will have any trouble correctly diagnosing an excess demand for cars. It presents itself in unmistakably clear terms. The car dealers will temporarily be out of stock, and they'll tell you that, although next month's shipment will be larger than this month's, each car will sell at a higher price than it did this month.

People have more trouble diagnosing an excess demand for money than they do an excess *demand* for cars because the excess demand for money doesn't present itself as an excess demand, but rather as an excess supply, of everything else. Both shut down producers and unemployed workers confront a lack of demand, for products in one case and for labor services in the other. But people don't find money holdings unavailable generally. If they had jobs and had customers, people (people individually, anyway) could hold as much money as they wanted to hold. But they don't have jobs, and they don't have customers. They'll just have to get along, then, with money balances smaller than they would otherwise like to hold.

Inflation

Too small a money supply shows itself as an excess supply of everything else. Too large a money supply shows itself as quite the opposite problem—an across-the-board excess demand for ordinary things. No one, however, in either case will see a monetary problem *per se*. In the excessdemand-for money case, people don't regard the asset money as generally unavailable; customers and willing-to-hire employers are scarce, not money. And even when an excess supply of money exists, money doesn't become generally unacceptable as the medium of exchange; nobody turns away paying customers or employers with paychecks in their hands.

Because money is the routine medium of exchange, then, people will always *accept* it, even if they have no intention of holding it. They accept the excess supply of money—actually, they have no choice, because refusing it would mean refusing to make ordinary sales—and then they just pass it along to someone else. It's easy enough to do, of course; just spend it.

Here, again, however, as in the depression case, individual and overall points of view diverge. Individually, everyone can get rid of money by just spending it; no one has to worry about getting stuck with it. The community as a whole, on the other hand, can't get rid of money by spending it; the community as a whole has to hold however much money actually exists, every last penny of it. Instead of reducing the total quantity of money, individually successful but collectively futile efforts to get rid of money have the effect of expanding the flows of spending and income and, ultimately, therefore, of reducing the purchasing power of the money unit.

The money unit's reduced purchasing power, the permanently higher general price level, eliminates the excess supply of money. The excess money doesn't disappear. Rather, the higher price level persuades people to absorb into money balances demanded what, initially, they considered too large a quantity of money. Larger money holdings give people the same degree of protection against that awkward moment when the unexpected but now, thanks to the higher prices, larger expense arises. The higher price level, then, is both the symptom of and the cure for the same problem—an excess supply of money.

Stagflation

Combining the ills of inflation *and* unemployment, stagflation might seem to pose a diagnostic challenge for macroeconomic theory. By working out an analogy between the difficulty of reducing the price level, on the one hand, and just moderating its rate of increase, on the other hand, however, we can extend the monetary disequilibrium theory to handle the supposedly more difficult to understand hybrid case.

An entrenched price level itself resists downward pressure because no one has adequate incentive to go first in what has to be, when it eventually occurs, a piecemeal adjustment process. But neither does anyone have adequate incentive to go first in moderating an entrenched rate of price inflation. Say that you've become accustomed to marking up your price by ten percent per year; you've done so routinely, year after year. Even in the face, now, of slackened demand for your product will you immediately alter your customary pricing behavior? Are you sure economic conditions won't soon revert to trend? Republishing merchandise catalogs, just to mention one obvious consideration, isn't cheap. And if you've accepted delivery of material at their already-marked-up prices, how can you afford not to mark up the price that you'll charge for your own finished product? Even if economic conditions really have permanently changed, why shouldn't your employees' labor union, whose leaders haven't recently had the chance to negotiate a new contract, get the pay raise that would enable its members to catch up with everyone else? All of these things tell in favor of a person's wanting to follow, not lead. It's hard to reduce the price-andwage level, once people have become accustomed to it; and, apparently, it's just as hard to reduce the price-and-wage level's rate of increase, once people have become accustomed to *it*.

Even when the government's changed economic policy reduces the money supply's inflationary growth rate, then, prices and wages will, for a while, anyway—exactly how long, it's very hard to say—continue to rise just as quickly as they've been rising all along. As long as prices and wages do continue rising at the customary rate, however, whatever the customary rate may be, the now more slowly growing quantity of money won't be large enough to satisfy the community's demand for money holdings. The monetary stringency will adversely affect production and employment now and only later, when economic pressures to alter pricing behavior have become sufficiently strong, moderate the rate of price-and-wage inflation instead. All the worse will these adverse effects be, of course, if the public perceives the government as irresolute and likely to revert to its inflationary ways.

Diagnosis: Money

Understandably, perhaps, because each of us specializes in producing one particular thing, we have a tendency to diagnose economic problems, however widespread they may be, as industry specific problems. When a problem is truly *macro*economic in nature, however, some very general and very basic imbalance must exist, an imbalance involving money, the one thing traded on *all* markets. Macroeconomic problems fall into three categories: depression, inflation, and stagflation. To an old-fashioned monetarist like me, economic depression means too little money, price inflation means too much money, and stagflation, the hybrid condition, means too little money now against a backdrop of too much money earlier.[1]

---

1 For the monetary theory and even some of the language that I've used in this chapter, I give credit to my long-time collaborator, Leland B. Yeager. His collected essays on monetary theory, including essays that we've written together, appear in George Selgin, ed., *The Fluttering Veil: Essays on Monetary Disequilibrium* by Leland B. Yeager (Indianapolis: Liberty Fund, 1997). See, too, Richard H. Timberlake's book review essay, *Cato Journal*, 1998, Spring, 156-62.

8

*Is Saving Really A Vice?**

Troubles Adjusting to College

I grew up in a home that considered saving an unquestioned virtue. At eighteen years old, however, having gone back to college for my sophomore year, I found both my macroeconomics professor and the textbook that he had assigned saying something far less complimentary about saving than my parents had said about it. Both the professor and the textbook said that, if people tried to save more, production and employment would suffer (not "could suffer", they said, but "would suffer"). Far from seeing saving as a virtue, I should now see it as a vice, public even if not private, the cause of economic depressions, including the Great Depression, which my parents themselves had lived through.

My days as an undergraduate are now more than thirty-five years behind me; yet some economists and textbooks teach this anti-saving lesson still, and all the more remarkably to judge by the 1980s and 1990s lament that we Americans save too little, that we concern ourselves too little with the future. I've since come to understand, however, that to explain economic depressions, we don't have to—nor should we—hand up a blanket indictment of thrift *per se*. Based loosely on the first of Sir Dennis Robertson's four, early 1931 BBC radio addresses, the following story aims at showing that what causes economic depressions isn't the public's wanting to save but rather a money supply inadequate to permit the public's thrifty intentions to bear fruit as real capital.

---

* This material appears in Roger Koppl, ed., *Money and Markets: Essays in Honor of Leland B. Yeager* (New York: Routledge, 2006), 143-50. The material is reproduced here, with permission.

Our One-Classroom Economy

My story begins. Here in our one-classroom economy, we five people work hard. We produce chairs—one chair each, let's say, per month, or 12 chairs per year. Each of the five of us, then, has a 12-chair real income flow per year. If we cared to do so, we could devote our entire 60 chair per year real income to current consumption; we could use the chairs in our dining rooms, on our patios, or wherever. If used now, each chair will last a year and then disappear.

Perhaps it's just in the nature of the human animal to crave what other people have; it's always somebody else's chair that appeals to us, and getting it requires trade. Conducting trade on the basis of barter, of course, would be inconvenient for everyone. Luckily, however, each one of us has a checking account with the one-classroom economy's only bank. You can sell a chair to one person, have the bank add the proceeds to your own account, and then, by writing a check yourself, buy a chair from someone else. We use no money other than the checking accounts issued by this—our one and only—bank.

Now there's no telling when you'll come across the chair of your dreams. It may happen when you have no chair to sell or when you just can't find anyone who wants to buy the chair you have. To make sure that you don't find yourself in such a circumstance, to make sure that you can buy a chair on even a moment's notice, you find it convenient to hold a checking-account balance that is roughly the equivalent of two months' income (i.e., two chairs), as does everyone else. All of your receipts and expenditures flow through your checking account balance, receipts enlarging that balance and expenditures reducing it. When, because you deposit a check your balance grows, someone else's balance falls, of course, and when, because you write a check your balance falls, someone else's balance rises.

Say that there exist 1,000 of these checking account dollars, total. Then, to make that 1,000-unit money supply the equivalent of two months' flow of dollar spending and income, the annual flow of dollar spending and income has to be $6,000. Each of the 60 chairs that we produce annually must therefore have a $100 price tag.

The Demand for Money and the Supply of Capital

Now, through immigration, let's say, our population doubles, from five people to ten. Like each of us old timers, each of the five newcomers can produce one chair per month, 12 per year, and, again like each old timer, each newcomer wants to hold a $200 checking-account balance, the equivalent of one-sixth of a year's income. With the newcomers' arrival, then, potential total real income jumps from 60 chairs per year to 120 chairs per year, and the aggregate demand for money balances grows from $1,000 to $2,000. To accumulate a $200 checking account balance, furthermore, each of the five newcomers is willing to make a one-time sacrifice of two months' income. The newcomers as a group, in other words, are willing to just hold the money that selling ten of their first year's 60 chairs brings in, instead of using that money to buy chairs for themselves. The newcomers' demand for money holdings, then, is actually an additional *supply* of real capital. By holding money, they relinquish the chairs that they could have bought with it. Thanks to the newcomers' thriftiness, those ten chairs sit poised, ready to become part of the economy's capital stock.

Now, at the very moment that our population doubles, I come up with a scheme for transforming an ordinary chair into something better, a chair that will last two years. Transforming ordinary chairs into new, improved chairs, however, requires my having ordinary chairs to work with—I need capital, real capital. Not wanting to devote my own chairs to the project or to borrow chairs from someone else directly, I go to the bank. I ask for a $1,000 loan. The bank consents and credits my checking account balance $1,000. With the newly created money, I buy ten chairs, plugging the hole in the spending stream that the five newcomers create by demanding checking account balances of their own. By demanding money balances of their own, then, the newcomers are committing ten chairs to the bank's care, and the bank, by creating new money on loan, transfers the ten chairs to me. My intended investment in chairs equals the newcomers' intended saving of chairs—or, what is the same thing, the total quantity of checking account money just satisfies the now enlarged community's total demand for holdings of checking-account money.

Forced Saving

There's no assurance, however, that plans will mesh as nicely as they did in this particular case. After all, the bank doesn't know what portion of their first year's chair production the newcomers want to give up as a means of acquiring checking account balances. The banker knows nothing about the demand for holdings of money. How could the banker know how many checks people plan to write and in what amounts they plan to write them? The banker deals with me, the borrower, but never actually speaks with the people who wind up holding the newly created money.

The community's not wanting to hold new money, however, can't block the bank from creating it. In a second version of the story, I might ask for and actually get a $2,000 loan. After I spend it, every checking account dollar that the bank creates to buy my promissory note denominated $2,000 has to wind up in *somebody's* account.On the bank's balance sheet, my $2,000 promissory note appears as an asset and, offsetting it, the community's checking accounts of $2,000 appear as liabilities.

Now, you people don't really want to add $2,000 to your holdings of checking account money; the new total quantity of checking account money, $3,000, is the equivalent of three months' income [($3,000/$12,000) x 12 months], not two months'. You have no choice, however, other than to accept the new money when it comes your way, because refusing to accept the money would mean refusing to make ordinary sales. You'll gladly accept the new money, planning to spend it away yourselves. Next day, when you go to the store, looking for chairs to buy, however, what will you find? You'll find ten fewer chairs than you want to buy, 100 chairs instead of 110. The bank, in effect, gives me, its borrower, the keys to the one-classroom economy's chair stores, and then, keys in hand, I beat the rest of you people to the chairs.

Instead of those ten chairs, then, you nine people get money. You wind up with ten chairs fewer than you find it desirable to use and $1,000 more money than you find it convenient to hold. The excess supply of money expands the annual flow of spending and income. The flow expands to $18,000 a year, once again making the bank's monetary liabilities, despite having grown to $3,000, the equivalent of two months' income.

The bank's loan assets must also be once again the equivalent of two months' income, and this balance sheet condition may seem to suggest that the bank cannot transfer to industry any more real capital (again, chairs) than the newcomers entrust to it voluntarily. But such a conclusion would be incorrect, of course, for the bank transfers to me, its borrower, not just the two months' income (ten chairs) that the newly enlarged community wants to part with but two more months' income (another ten chairs) besides. Increased money holdings give concrete evidence of the community's having saved twenty chairs. One-half of that saving, however, thanks to the bank's intervention, is saving that you do not voluntarily, but under duress.

Without the bank's intervention, I would have to use my own chairs as capital, or else, to finance the chair improvement scheme, approach you directly and, by offering a higher interest rate on my promissory notes, *persuade* you to lend me your chairs. With the bank's intervention, however, I can inflict forced saving upon you, but no trace of it shows up on the bank's balance sheet. Like the cat sleeping innocently before the kitchen stove after already having swallowed the canary, the bank's balance sheet gives no hint that something is amiss.

Wasted Saving

It was with a concern with the opposite case, however, that this story began: the bird escapes the cat's clutches and then heads right out the open window, gone forever.

The wasted saving case begins in the same way that the two preceding cases began: each of our five newcomers wants to hold a $200 checking-account balance, the equivalent of two months' income; I come up with a scheme for transforming an ordinary chair, which if used now will last just one year, into something better, a chair that will last two years; and again, needing capital, I go to the bank. This time, however, I'm not quite as confident in my abilities. I ask for and get just a $500 loan—not enough money to enable me to take over all ten of the chairs that the five newcomers want to relinquish in favor of money holdings, but only five of those sacrificial chairs. The excess of the newcomers' intended chair saving over my chair investment, or, what is the same thing, the community's excess demand for holdings of checking-account money, doesn't show up on the bank's books. The bank's loan assets are, as they must always be, exactly equal to its deposit liabilities. The intended saving — intended investment imbalance shows up again, as it does in the case of forced saving, not at the bank but on the chair market. The excess demand for money holdings has as its other and more plainly visible side an excess supply of chairs.

The visibility of the chair market and the temptation to apply supply-and-demand-type thinking to it might suggest that the price of chairs would just fall, thereby bringing the supply of and demand for chairs (and thus supply of and demand for money balances) back into line with each other rather quickly and painlessly. Perhaps the price *would* just fall if a chair were really a chair and nothing else. "A chair", however, is just a metaphor for what in reality, outside the one-classroom economy, are quantities of different goods and services, and the chair's "price", therefore, a metaphor for the general price level.

Despite the excess supply of chairs, then, their price won't fall quickly and easily. It's hard to get the general price level down because, for a while, anyway, until pressure builds sufficiently and someone has no choice but to succumb, the who-goes-first problem blocks the downward adjustment. Lacking assurance that suppliers and competitors will follow suit by cutting their own prices, no chair producer wants to take the lead in what, when eventually it happens, has to be a piecemeal and decentralized downward adjustment. At a price now too high for equilibrium but resisting downward adjustment, therefore, the excess supply of metaphorical chairs persists.

There the other five chairs just sit, then, gathering dust, going to waste. More likely, because they can't be sold, those other five chairs won't even be produced. The resources that would have been used to produce them will wind up unemployed, and from there the waste will very likely spread (though not spread limitlessly, because as money holdings became too large in relation to incomes shrunken any further, spending would resume).

Money, Saving, and Investment

Case	Intended Saving	Investment	Actual Saving	Change, Capital Stock	Quantity of Money
Equilibrium	10 chairs	10 chairs	10 chairs	10 chairs	Correct
Forced Saving (Inflation)	10 chairs	20 chairs	20 chairs	20 chairs	Excess Supply: $1000
Wasted Saving (Recession)	10 chairs	5 chairs	5 chairs	5 chairs	Excess Demand: $500

The bank, in this case, has failed to translate the newcomers' intended saving into real capital. We shouldn't be overly hard on the bank, however, despite its having failed to translate the newcomers' intended saving into real capital. After all, savers commit their chairs to the bank's care by simply exercising restraint in spending—by writing fewer checks against the bank and writing those fewer checks in smaller denominations, too. The bank has no way of gauging the savers' thrifty intentions, however, and therefore doesn't know that, by creating new money on loan, it should make available to chair investors all of the furniture relinquished voluntarily by the savers.

If our newly arrived savers had wanted to hold promissory notes themselves, bonds, not checking account money, then intended saving could not have gone to waste. The increased demand for bond holdings would have driven their interest yield down. By encouraging otherwise hesitant investors to try their hands at the chair improvement scheme (and perhaps even discouraging otherwise willing savers from releasing their chairs), the lower interest rate on the bonds would have directly eliminated chair investment's shortfall beneath the community's intended chair saving.

No such automatic adjustment occurs, however, when savers want to hold actual money. In contrast with the demand for holdings of bonds, the demand for holdings of money doesn't register on any particular market. The quantity of money, in other words, is not supply-and-*demand* determined. The bank creates money almost unintentionally, through its lending operations. If, as in the wasted saving case, the bank through its lending operations creates a quantity of money smaller than the public wants to hold, people don't go to the bank, asking to borrow money. Instead, to get the money that they want to hold, people just passively curtail their spending. Curtailed spending, together with the general price level's understandable tendency to resist downward pressure, creates depressed economic conditions.

Depressed economic conditions do not mean that the public is actually *doing* too much saving. Quite to the contrary, depressed economic conditions mean that, constrained by too small a quantity of money, the public can't do *as much* saving as it would otherwise like to do.

To Sum Up

For his 1931 BBC listeners, Dennis Robertson, himself a master of verbal imagery, summed up this way. "[S]ome-times," Sir Dennis said, "there is a whole host of borrowers ringing at the front bell—Mr. Farmer, Mr. Merchant, Mr. Manufacturer and the rest; and Mrs. Thrift sitting within the parlour, has forgotten to order any food. So the parlourmaid has to keep the crowd from the door—by sharp words, by raising the standard of the tips she demands, by any device that occurs to her. And sometimes there is tea laid for fifty, and nobody calls, and all the good food is wasted: for the parlourmaid has been strictly brought up, and knows, or think she knows, that she ought not to give food away to casual passers by."[1]

The attentive listener must surely have understood what Sir Dennis meant. Sir Dennis's head parlourmaid was "the old lady of Threadneedle Street", the Bank of England; in Robertson's "and nobody calls" case— 1931—the Bank had let the weakened demand for loans beguile her into thinking that her hands were tied. But her hands weren't tied at all. The Bank could have and should have found a way to get new money into the public's hands and, by so doing, kept all of Mrs. Thrift's good food from being wasted.

---

1   For a complete transcription of Robertson's four 1931 BBC radio broadcasts, see Dennis H. Robertson and A.C. Pigou, *Economic Essays and Addresses* (London: P.S. King, 1931), 183-215

9

Money Here Today (1929) but Gone Tomorrow (1933)

Self-Restraint?

Economic depression is the painfully visible side of an excess demand for holdings of money balances. But if, as the preceding chapter's story teaches, what we use as money comes into existence as a result of the bank's lending, one has to wonder. Is there a banker alive who, if given the opportunity to print money, would exhibit the self-restraint needed to produce a *deficiency* of money?

Actually, to explain the monetary deficiency, it isn't to the banker's self-restraint that we should look. We should look, instead, to an externally imposed restraint. This chapter's story explains the nature of the external restraint and then offers the period 1929-1933 as an illustration of how severely the restraint has sometimes been made to work.

Money Here Today (1929)

To avoid unnecessary complications, I assume, again, the existence of just a single bank. Its balance sheet shows that the bank's $900 loan to business and its $100 loan to the government have created the community's checking account balances of $1,000.

Banking System

Assets		Liabilities
Loans	$1,000	Checking Accounts $1,000
To Business	$900	
To Government	100	

Like any other borrower, of course, the government would prefer not to see the day when its debt to the bank comes due. It can put that day off indefinitely by telling the bank that, if it wants to continue using the word "bank", it must hold among its assets green paper receipts, each receipt bearing the likeness of a former president or other American dignitary. The denominations of the receipts, the government might say, must total at least 10 percent of the bank's checking account liabilities.

In our story, the bank has already issued 1,000 checking account dollars and therefore must hold Federal Reserve receipts denominated, in total, $100. To get them, the authorities say, the bank must hand over to the Federal Reserve evidence of the government's $100 debt. Once in the Federal Reserve's possession, the government's bond is effectively retired, because unlike the bank, the Federal Reserve will not insist that the U.S. Treasury make good on it. On the bank's balance sheet, non-interest bearing Federal Reserve receipts take the government bond's place.

Banking System				Federal Reserve	
Assets		Liabilities	Assets		Liabilities
Deposit with	$100	Checking Accounts $1,000	Government Bonds $100		Deposit of Bank $100
Federal Reserve					
Loans	900				
To Business	$900				
To Government	0				

Reluctantly, then, the bank gives up the bond and in return for it gets the Federal Reserve receipts with denominations totaling $100. If the bank wants it to do so, the Federal Reserve, instead of printing paper receipts, will just add the same total to a deposit liability that it maintains in the bank's name. Later, if the bank wants all or some of its paper receipts actually printed up and delivered to it, perhaps to pay out over its counter for the public to use as pocket cash, then they're just a telephone call and an armored car drive away. In terms of keeping the bank legal, the bank's deposit balance with the Federal Reserve is every bit as good as cash sitting in the bank's vault.

...*But Gone Tomorrow (1933)*

The quantity of Federal Reserve receipts sitting in the bank's vault or, as we're now telling the story, just credited to the bank's account with the Federal Reserve anchors the quantity of checking account money; a 10:1 gearing links the public's checking account balances to the bank's Federal Reserve receipts. The bank may, for example, find itself called upon to release some of its cash. To make cash available and at the same time comply with the required 10:1 gearing, the bank must extinguish ten checking account dollars (liabilities) for each cash dollar (assets) that it loses. To extinguish checking account dollars, the bank calls in loans, which the former borrowers repay by writing checks against the bank itself. Calling in loans doesn't actually provide the bank any new cash. Instead, by extinguishing deposits, calling in loans makes cash that the bank already has dispensable.

In late 1928, preoccupied with the speculative frenzy that had the New York stock market in its grip and having judged its policy too expansive and thus responsible for the stock-market speculation, the Federal Reserve began taking cash out of the banking system. At prices that people found irresistibly low, the Federal Reserve sold off Treasury obligations that it had been holding itself. To take payment on the checks that the buyers wrote when they bought the U.S. government bonds, the Federal Reserve reduced its own deposit liability to the bank. The bank lost one cash dollar for every checking account dollar that a depositor used to buy a government bond from the Federal Reserve. But extinguishing one checking account dollar wasn't sufficient. Because the gearing ratio is ten (checking account dollars) to one (cash dollar), nine more checking account dollars had to go, too. The bank called in a $9 loan, then, and the former borrower repaid the loan by writing a $9 check against the bank. To pay the Federal Reserve the $1 cash, the bank had to shrink the public's checking account balances by $10.

Between 1928 and 1930, the Federal Reserve extinguished checking account money by selling bonds and then, to take payment on the checks used to pay for them, canceling as much of the bank's cash. After late 1930, however, though with the same multiplied effect on checking account money, the cash walked right out the bank's front door. Skittish depositors descended upon the bank, insisting that the bank convert checking account dollars into cash dollars. It made no difference where the cash dollar went—to the Federal Reserve (as when a depositor bought a bond from the Federal Reserve) or to a depositor (when a depositor withdrew cash); for every cash dollar that the bank lost it had to extinguish ten checking account dollars. The bond purchase or the cash withdrawal extinguished the first cash dollar. Nine other checking account dollars disappeared when the bank called in a $9 loan and the borrower, to meet the bank's call for repayment, wrote a check that size against the bank. The bank runs thus tended to shrink the money supply by several times the bank's loss of cash.

The three waves of bank runs didn't cause the bank as great a net loss of cash, and therefore didn't cause as great a cancellation of bank money, however, as they might have caused. Briefly, anyway, the Federal Reserve reversed course and began again buying government bonds. Sellers deposited the Federal Reserve's checks, and by sending the checks right back to the Federal Reserve, the bank got paper money that it could then pay out over the counter. The bank didn't have to unlock this cash: it didn't have to shrink checking accounts by more than the cash being withdrawn. The bank runs didn't have as great a direct effect on the money supply, then, as they might have had.

Indirectly, however, and even apart from the bank's failing outright, the runs took an enormous toll on the quantity of checking account money. The nervous banker decided that the 10 (checking account dollars):1 (cash dollar) gearing ratio was too risky; the ratio 5:1 sounded better—safer. Now, for every ten checking account dollars in circulation, each one of the checking account dollars a threat to the bank's reserves, the banker wanted not one but two cash dollars sitting in the vault or within reach, anyway, by telephone.

The banker wanted to reduce the gearing ratio, but the banker couldn't create the cash that it would have taken to effect the desired reduction. Reducing the ratio meant shrinking deposits relative to whatever cash the bank still had. By March 1933, more than 25 percent of the country's money supply had just vanished. The last chapter of the Depression's shrunken-money-supply story, furthermore, was a chapter destined to repeat itself. In 1935, the Federal Reserve would notice that our bank held excess cash reserves and therefore, to prevent what it worried would become "an uncontrollable expansion of credit in the future",[1] would over the next two years double the reserve-requirement ratio. But would the bank in 1935 really have excess reserves? To the bank, they wouldn't seem excessive at all. Having seen rough times, the bank would consider it prudent to hold reserves above and beyond what the law required. The bank would regain the lower ratio, as before, by shrinking deposit liabilities. The money supply would shrink, and the years 1937 and 1938 would bring with them a return to something much like the depressed economic conditions of the years 1929 through 1933.

The Great Depression

By March 1933, when the economy hit its first 1930s trough, one-quarter of the total 1929 money supply had just vanished. This shrinkage, however, actually understates the effective shortage of money. An effective shortage would have developed even if the money supply had remained constant because, to grow—to accommodate an increased population, for example—the economy needs additional money. The effective shrinkage, calculated as the shortage beneath the money supply's 1923-1928 trend extended to 1933, stood at roughly one third.

The 1933 quantity of money was far too small a quantity, then, to satisfy the public's full-employment demand for holdings of the medium of exchange. The 1933 quantity of the monetary lubricant was therefore far too small to keep the underlying system of producing goods and services and then exchanging them for other goods and services going. Of these ordinary goods and services, excess supplies were everywhere, and all too painfully, apparent.

The excess supplies of goods and services began working to push prices down and thus, by making an initially too small nominal money supply larger in real terms, began working to eliminate the excess demand for money holdings. Prices did fall, but for understandable reasons only sluggishly. Their sluggish response explains why reduced money incomes, required by the now much reduced money supply, came in the especially unpleasant form of reduced annual production (one third beneath 1929's level) and therefore an increased unemployment rate (upwards of 20 percent).

---

1 *Annual Report of the Board of Governors of the Federal Reserve System*, 1935,

Among the public, furthermore, lower prices, when eventually they came, bred expectations of still lower prices. People didn't rush to spend their money; they held it, expecting to get even better bargains later on. Money's velocity fell, in other words, necessitating a still greater reduction of money incomes, and for full employment, therefore, a still sharper fall in prices.

Then, too, and to make things still worse, lower prices made existing debts, fixed as of course they were in dollar terms, harder for people to repay. Large and small, businesses and homes were dragged under by a tidal wave of bankruptcies.

Benjamin Strong

Why didn't the Federal Reserve act to prevent the downturn of 1929 from becoming the Great Depression? One answer to this question centers on a particular person, Benjamin Strong.

Nowadays, of course, when we think of the Federal Reserve and monetary policy, we think of Washington, D.C., where the Federal Reserve System's Board of Governors sits. The more youthful Federal Reserve, however, had a different center of influence. The system's center of influence was the Federal Reserve Bank of New York, and Benjamin Strong, the person who then headed the New York Bank, the system's most influential person. First in 1924 and then again in 1927, Strong used his influence to very good purpose. With the Federal Reserve Board's approval (its consent wasn't required), he had the New York Bank buy government bonds, and those purchases nipped two mild recessions in the bud. Strong might have done the same thing again, in 1929, had he lived to witness that business downturn and the deep depression that followed it. But Strong died in 1928, of tuberculosis.

Irving Fisher, whom some people consider not just America's first great economist but still, even to this day, America's greatest economist, concluded in 1935 that Benjamin Strong's death had made an independent contribution to what became the Great Depression. "I thoroughly believe," wrote Fisher, "that if he had lived and his policies been continued, we might have had the stock market crash in milder form, but after the crash there would not have been the great industrial depression."[2] Thirty years

2 Irving Fisher. "Reflation and Stabilization", and "Discussion", *Annals of the American Academy of Political and Social Science*, 1934, Janaury, 127-31, 151.

later, in *A Monetary History of the United States*, Milton Friedman and Anna J. Schwartz would agree with Fisher. Nor, over the years, would their view change. "We continue to believe," Schwartz says, "that had Strong lived or had he been succeeded by someone of similar views and equal personal force, the same monetary growth policies followed in 1924 and 1927 would have been followed in 1930...and the economy would have been spared its prolonged ordeal."[3]

Friedman and Schwartz take special notice of the diminished position that the New York Bank assumed after Strong's passing. In central banking circles, people aspire to the title Governor, and originally, together with just one person in Washington, D.C., each of the twelve regional Federal Reserve banks had someone wearing that special mantle. Culminating a political struggle that began with Strong's death, an act of 1935 demoted each Federal Reserve Bank's governor, including the governor of the New York Bank, to president. The Federal Reserve System itself now had a full Board of Governors, sitting in Washington, D.C., and together with representatives of five among the System's twelve regional Banks (New York's representative as a permanent member and four other Banks' representatives on a rotating basis), each of the Board's seven members sat on the reorganized Open Market Policy Committee.

Even earlier, however, that committee's predecessor, the Open Market Investment Committee, had been expanded to include not just representatives of the New York and four other eastern Federal Reserve Banks but representatives of all twelve regional Banks. In decisions concerning open-market operations, therefore, the New York Bank had lost influence. Officials of the New York Bank, according to Friedman and Schwartz, argued for aggressive monetary policy to combat the depression, but on the expanded committee, the New York Bank didn't have the votes. Like Fisher, then, Friedman and Schwartz see Strong's passing, in 1928, as a watershed. His passing and the New York Bank's reduced influence they regard as not just untimely but actually, for the country and indeed the world, tragic.

But even some economists who, like Fisher and like Friedman and Schwartz, give the Great Depression a monetary diagnosis, don't think

---

3 Anna J. Schwartz, "Understanding 1929-1933", in her *Money in Historical Perspective* (Chicago: University of Chicago Press, 1987).

that Strong would have done in the 1930s what he had done in the two earlier recessions. Karl Brunner and Allan Meltzer, for example, see no principled contrast between the 1924 and 1927 policy on the one hand and the 1930s policy on the other hand. Relatively high interest rates and our bank's heavy indebtedness to the Federal Reserve, they say, triggered Strong's 1924 and 1927 open-market purchases of government bonds. In the 1930s case, according to Brunner and Meltzer, Strong would not have intervened with open-market purchases because he would have taken the relatively *low* interest rates and our bank's being only *slightly* indebted to the Federal Reserve to mean that we didn't need additional reserves. For the restrictive monetary policy after Strong's death, the level of interest rates and the state of our bank's indebtedness to the Federal Reserve are all the explanation required. "A special explanation of monetary policy after 1929," Brunner and Meltzer say, "is unnecessary."[4]

Fisher and also Friedman and Schwartz see Strong's death as marking a discernible change in monetary policy. Brunner and Meltzer, however, deny the contrast. The two camps differ on the "what would Benjamin Strong have done" question. For the Great Depression itself, however, they both blame the monetary contraction.

A Concluding Quotation

I conclude this chapter's story by quoting the recently surfaced July 23, 1946, letter from Irving Fisher to Clark Warburton. Warburton was an FDIC economist. His painstaking (and with his employer very unpopular) statistical work in the 1940s and 1950s laid at the Federal Reserve's door blame for business fluctuations in general and for the Great Depression specifically.[5] Warburton's research encouraged the next generation of economists to give the monetary theory of business fluctuations, a theory unfashionable in Warburton's own time, a new lease on life.

---

4 See Karl Brunner and Allan Meltzer, "What Did We Learn from the Monetary Experience of the United States during the Great Depression?" *Canadian Journal of Economics, 1968, May, 334-48 and Meltzer's A History of the Federal Reserve* (Chicago: University of Chicago Press, 2003), Vol. 1, Ch. 5.

5 For a collection of Warburton's published articles, see Clark Warburton, *Depression, Inflation, and Monetary Policy: Selected Papers*, 1945-1953 (Baltimore: Johns Hopkins University Press, 1966). On Warburton himself, see Leland B. Yeager, "Clark Warburton, 1896-1979", History of Political Economy, 1981, Summer, 279-84.

Fisher's 1946 letter to Warburton casts doubt on whether the Depression-era Federal Reserve even thought about "monetary policy", as such. "In the summer of 1931," Fisher told Warburton, "I called on Eugene Meyer, the chairman of the Federal Reserve board. I said: 'I am getting alarmed to see demand deposits diminish. It seems to me that this may make great trouble.' He said: 'What did you call that figure?' Amazed, I said: 'The full name is individual deposits subject to check without notice.' He rang a bell and asked his assistant to bring in the last controller's report open to the page where the figures were…. In a few minutes the report came in and I pointed and said: 'You see that…there has been a continuous reduction?' He said, 'Yes, I see.'"[6]

Apparently, as a numerical magnitude, the money supply wasn't much on the Federal Reserve's mind. I'd like to say that only Federal Reserve officials were in this way neglectful. I'm afraid, however, that there's more than enough blame to go around, even—or should I say *especially?*—among economists. As an economist who saw the quantity of money as a critical magnitude, Irving Fisher seems to have been very much in the minority.

---

6 Thomas Cargill, "Irving Fisher Comments on Benjamin Strong and the Federal Reserve in the 1930s", *Journal of Political Economy*, 1992, December, 1275-76.

10
Golden Rules of the Depression Era

On the subject of gold, Edwin Cannan, a founder of the London School of Economics, came right to the point. "The greatest obstacle to the adoption...of sound policy," Cannan said, "is the exaggerated belief in gold as a sign of national wealth and prosperity which has come down to us as a legacy from the mercantilist period.... People rejoice when they hear of an import of gold...and deplore any export of it...not [, however,] because they recognize that gold is a metal with many useful properties, and expect that it will, when imported, serve purposes which will delight the eye. So much of it as goes to such purposes they consider little better than wasted. What they like to hear is that gold has been 'secured', as the financial editors call it, by the central bank and is about to be immured in that bank's deepest dungeon for ever and ever, amen."[1] Such, it seems, was the mystique of gold, and not just in England.

The Federal Reserve and other central banks, most notably the Bank of France, were locked in a competitive struggle for gold. Together, in 1931, these two central banks held 64 percent of the world's monetary gold stock. The worldwide scramble for gold meant that gold had to become more valuable relative to goods and services in general: either the price of gold had to rise or all other prices had to fall. The mystique of gold made governments hesitant about raising the official price of gold. The alternative was a general deflation. The painful process of getting national price levels down and then coping with the results of their having fallen was the Great Depression.

---

1 Edwin Cannan, *Modern Currency and Regulation of Its Value* (London: P.S. King & Son, 1931), 69-70.

Fisher's Compensated-Dollar Rule

Even before the Depression, Irving Fisher, the famous Yale economist, recognized the problem. As the medium of exchange, gold had long since been replaced by banknotes and deposits. Gold still served as the standard of value, but Fisher saw that we could do better than using a single commodity, especially gold, as the standard of value.

Fisher had a plan.[2] It resembled an ordinary gold standard in that the Federal Reserve would redeem the dollar for and also issue it against a particular quantity of gold. Fisher's plan differed from an ordinary gold standard, however, in that the specified quantity of gold would be changed every two months or so to counteract any movement that the general level of prices might have shown. For $1, the Federal Reserve would buy or sell gold in the quantity that, at the most recent observation of prices, had the same dollar value as some comprehensive basket of goods.

To take a simple example of how Fisher's plan would work, say that for $1 you could buy either an ounce of gold or the comprehensive market basket itself. Suppose, now, that the basket's composite price rose to $2. To counteract the doubling of the basket's composite price, the authorities would double the dollar's gold content. For $1, in other words, the Federal Reserve would now give you two ounces of gold, which you then could sell for $2; and for the $2, the Federal Reserve would give you four ounces of gold, which you then could sell for $4. Even if the price of gold itself doubled when the basket's composite price doubled, profit would be there just for the taking. For $1, the Federal Reserve would still have to give you gold worth $2, and then for $2, gold worth $4. With each round the money supply would shrink, and the resulting dampened spending would reverse the assumed increase of the basket's composite price.

Fisher's plan would have had to prohibit the Federal Reserve from holding gold reserves. Suppose that, because the basket's price rose to $2, the Federal Reserve redeemed $1 in two ounces of gold that it released from its own reserves. The Federal Reserve would be charging $.50 per ounce of gold. That lower "price" would become the market price, and before actually redeeming money, the Federal Reserve would have to

---

2 Irving Fisher, *The Purchasing Power of Money* (New York: Macmillan, 1912 (1922)), *Stabilizing the Dollar* (New York: Macmillan, 1920), and *Stable Money: A History of the Movement* (New York: Adelphi, 1934). Irving N. Fisher, *My Father, Irving Fisher* (New York: Comet Press Books, 1956).

recalculate the quantity of gold to be handed over. Each calculation, because it reduced the market price, would require re-calculation and thus establish a lower price. Money redemptions touched off by a movement of the basket's composite price above $1 could send the price of gold falling to zero. To prevent its redemption price from dominating the market price, the Federal Reserve would have to redeem money, therefore, whenever it did so, by handing over gold that it bought on the market after selling off some other asset. The redemption operation would add as much to the demand for gold, then, as it did to the supply, leaving the market price of gold unchanged but shrinking the money supply to reverse any inflation of the general price level.

Next, to see how the compensated-dollar plan would work to counteract deflation, let's imagine that the basket's composite price fell from $1 to $.50, and perhaps the price of gold, too, along with it. Gold that you could buy for $.50 would now, when presented at the Federal Reserve's redemption-andissue window, get you $1. (To keep the Federal Reserve's price from dominating the market price, the plan would require the Federal Reserve to sell off the newly acquired gold and then use the proceeds to buy something else.) With the newly issued $1, you could buy two ounces of gold, against which the Federal Reserve then would issue $2. The quantity of money would grow. The enlarged quantity of money would trigger increased spending, reversing the assumed drop in the basket's composite price.

Fisher's original plan assigned to gold the role of redemption medium. This assignment, however, was really just a public relations gimmick. Fisher understood that without a part for gold, his plan wouldn't get a serious hearing. But even with the public relations gimmick, the plan didn't sell. Fisher became the target of much ridicule, in fact, as the proponent of what his critics called "a rubber dollar".

Fisher understood, of course, that the real objective was not the compensated dollar *per se* but managing the money supply to stabilize the general price level. To this end, he helped draft what, in March 1932, became known as the Goldsborough bill—H.R.7895: A Bill to Provide for the Stabilization of the Price Level for Commodities in General. After being reported favorably out of the House Banking Committee, the bill got the full House's approval. On the Senate side, however, the Goldsborough bill languished, and eventually died, in committee.

FDR's Golden Rule

Even if not the result of decreased output and hence unemployment but instead the result of just lower prices and wages, decreased income makes debts, fixed in dollar terms, harder to repay. If debtors default, creditors, who have debts of their own to repay, default, too. Bankruptcy is a highly contagious affliction.

The Depression-era contagion of deflation-induced bankruptcy had become so severe that, in March 1933, shortly after taking office, President Roosevelt declared it his intention to raise American prices back to where they had stood in 1926 and then to keep them there. The president's two sharply worded communiqués that summer to the World Monetary and Economic conference, which had set realigning exchange rates among gold-backed currencies as its chief objective, helped bring the conference to premature adjournment. "The revaluation of the dollar in terms of American commodities," Roosevelt declared in his second communiqué to London, "is an objective from which the government and the people of the United States cannot be diverted. We wish to make this perfectly clear: we are interested in American commodity prices. What is to be the value of the dollar in terms of foreign currencies is not and cannot be our immediate concern."

His two communiqués might seem to have suggested that President Roosevelt would use the weight of his office, together with his own personal influence, to get the U.S. money supply back on track. Actually, the messages meant something far different. Roosevelt had fallen under the influence of a Cornell agricultural economist, George Warren. Together with Frank Pearson, Warren had written a book arguing that it wasn't the quantity of money that determined the price level, but the *quantity of gold that each unit of money contained.*[3] The less gold each dollar contained, or would buy, Warren and Pearson's book said, the higher general prices would be. And that's exactly what President

---

3 George F. Warren and Frank A. Pearson, *Prices* (New York: Wiley, 1933).

Roosevelt wanted, higher prices. In October 1933, then, to raise the dollar price of gold and thereby in effect reduce the dollar's gold content, the Roosevelt administration began buying gold.

Warren and Pearson's thinking that the price level should mimic the price of gold harked back to the ancient doctrine of metallism. In olden times, of course, money wasn't just backed by gold; it actually was *gold*, a gold coin. Say, then, that because he didn't like the look or the feel of the gold coin, the king of olden times recalled all of the coins and then melted them down. And say that from this great mass of metal, the king struck the same number of coins as he had collected, each coin, however, now containing only 50 percent as much metal as it formerly contained. After finishing the job, the scrupulous king, let's suppose, sent the debased coins, denominations unchanged, back to their owners and then just held on to the surplus metal.

The coins would now be half their former gold weight. What should we expect would happen to prices? According to Warren and Pearson, prices would double. Their inflationary conclusion implies that, before making an offer for, say, a suit, the king's subjects pause to think about its value in relation to gold specifically. If in relation to gold, the suit hadn't become any more or any less appealing to people, then the suit would cost twice as many gold coins as before because each coin contained just half as much metal as it did before. Only a doubled price in gold coins would keep the suit's price in terms of gold unchanged.

Well, if Warren and Pearson's inflationary conclusion holds for gold coins, then shouldn't it hold for paper notes, too? What would happen to prices if the U.S. government recalled every Federal Reserve note, cut each note in half, and returned one half, still denominated one dollar, five dollars, ten dollars, or whatever, to its owner. Before making an offer for a suit, for example, would people weigh the suit against paper on their personal value scales and then, if the suit-versus-paper balance hadn't changed, offer for the suit twice as many paper dollars as before? Would the general price level rise if the Federal Reserve reduced the paper content of the dollar?

With respect to the general price level, the physical size of the new Federal Reserve note wouldn't matter. The key would be what the Federal Reserve did with the leftover paper (the leftover gold, in the first story). If the Federal Reserve added all the leftover paper to the money supply, then prices would rise to twice their former level, yes. They'd do so, however, not because each note contained just half as much paper as it did before, but because there would be twice as many notes in circulation as there had been before. If, on the other hand, the authorities cut the notes in half, reissued them at their former denominations, and then just held on to the leftover paper, then the price level wouldn't change.

Holding on to the leftover paper is, in effect, what the Roosevelt Administration did under its golden rule. To buy gold, in other words, instead of using newly printed money, the government used either tax receipts or borrowed money. Because it left the U.S. money supply unchanged, the devaluation of the dollar was sterilized of its across-the-board inflationary potential. Only certain prices rose, the prices of internationally traded goods—wheat, for example—prices that the Warren-Pearson price index, it turns out, weighted rather heavily.[4] These prices would indeed be expected to rise as the U.S. dollar weakened, as it did after April 1933.

The U.S. government closed its gold window in April 1933. Until January 1934, when the government reopened the gold window (at $35 per ounce, however, not the old $20.67), the fluctuating price of gold was the exchange rate between the paper dollar and currencies issued by governments that hadn't suspended their promises to buy and sell gold at fixed domestic currency prices. The more expensive in dollars gold became, then, the cheaper American wheat looked abroad to people who had gold or, more likely, had currencies that the issuing governments were still keeping convertible into gold; and the added demand abroad for the American wheat raised its dollar price. To compensate for wheat's higher price, however, other prices had to fall, because the U.S. money supply hadn't grown and therefore couldn't support a higher general price level. It was a fallacy to think that, merely as a consequence of gold's higher price, the entire U.S. price level would rise.

Especially when it comes to money, it seems, old fallacies die very hard. Every now and again, the editors of *The Wall Street Journal*, for example, will rediscover their own version of the Warren-Pearson doctrine. They'll claim that the government's buying and selling foreign currency in whatever quantities it takes to keep the dollar's exchange

---

4 George F. Warren and Frank A. Pearson, *Prices* (New York: Wiley, 1933).

rate unchanged will make the U.S. money supply correct.[5] Now, it's true that excessive money creation will cause the currency's foreign-exchange value to fall (or, under a fixed exchange rate, cause the country to run a cash deficit in its balance of payments). It doesn't follow, however, that every time the currency weakens (or, again, under a fixed exchange rate, the country runs a cash deficit in its balance of payments), too big a money supply has to be the cause. If, to keep the dollar from weakening, the government sells foreign currency at huge bargains, people will be more than happy to buy it. And they'll no less happily buy bonds if, hoping to keep the interest rate from falling, the government offers to sell *them* at bargain basement prices.

In both cases, the domestic money supply shrinks because the government, the issuer of the money, happens to be the seller. Its shrinking, however, hardly proves that the money supply was too big to start with. All the shrinkage proves is that, to get a bargain—in foreign exchange, in bonds, in anything else—people have to spend money, the actual medium of exchange. If the seller is an issuer of money, then the money that the buyers pay for these things gets canceled. The exchange rate (or, again, under a fixed exchange rate, the cash account in the balance of payments) is not a price test of the money supply's correctness. But neither is the interest rate on bonds, the *Journal's* other favorite criterion, a price test of its correctness. There is no price test of the money supply's correctness, because as the general medium of exchange, money lacks a market and therefore lacks a price distinctly its own.

China's Silver Shield

Under the gold standard, one country's deflating meant that, to continue pegging their currencies to gold, other countries had to follow suit. In short order, the depression that began here in the United States had spread throughout the gold bloc. By 1930 and with its hyperinflation, 19221924, still a fresh memory, Germany, for example, found itself mired in mass unemployment. A few countries escaped the Depression-era paralysis that had the gold bloc in its grip—China was

---

5 For some 1990s examples, see Greenfield *Monetary Policy and the Depressed Economy— As Illustrated by the Period 1929-1933,*(Belmont, CA: Wadsworth, 1994), 63. See, too, Bennett T. McCallum, "The *Wall Street Journal* Position on Exchange Rates", Shadow Open Market Committee Report (University of Rochester), April 2002.

the most populous such country—because they linked their currencies to silver, not gold.

Throughout the gold standard world, prices were falling, including the price of silver. Silver gravitated toward China, therefore, because the Chinese government hadn't changed the metal's official yuan price. Now with Chinese yuan to sell, foreign silver exporters and Chinese silver importers put downward exchange-market pressure on the yuan, and the currency's weakening permitted China to export goods as required to pay for the imported silver. Against the world's Great Depression, China, whose money supply grew, had a silver shield.

But China's silver shield would soon lose its effectiveness. In late 1931, several countries, including Britain, left gold and, by giving up gold, they relieved some of the pressure working to push gold price levels down. Then, in late 1933, the U.S. government, according to its long established political tradition of wanting "to do something for silver", began buying the metal, and silver's price in particular began to recover. Silver now flowed out of China, and as it did the Chinese money supply shrank. Even as some other countries began showing signs of economic recovery, therefore, China sank into depression.

Eventually, in 1935, China cut the yuan's link to silver. The world would head toward its second Great War and China, after the war, toward revolution and hyperinflation.[6]

---

6 On China, see Milton Friedman, "FDR, China, and Silver", in his *Money Mischief: Episodes in Monetary History* (New York: Harcourt Brace & Co., 1992), 157-88.

11

A Wartime Story of Government Finance

This chapter takes as its main business answering the two-fold question "What, as a nation, did the United States pay to defeat its World War II enemies and how, apart from conscription, which at one point had almost 12 million Americans under arms, did the nation marshal resources to the cause?" The analysis rests on five principles of economics, and these five principles are best stated, even if rather quickly, at the very outset.

First, individuals earn incomes that, in total, correspond to the whole national product. Second, the government's using a portion of the national product requires that the public relinquish an equally large portion of it. Third, the public's paying taxes and its accumulating government bonds and government-issued money are the financial side of transferring those real resources. Fourth, if banks hold as assets not the promissory notes of private borrowers but either cash reserves or government bonds, then together with cash in actual circulation, checking account balances, too, qualify as government-issued money. And fifth, if persuading the public to hold new money requires a higher price level, then the new money balances count not as evidence of voluntary saving but as receipts recording the public's having paid an implicit tax on holding money. These, then, are the five principles. Next comes their application to the World War II era.

For the United States, World War II began December 7, 1941, with the attack on Pearl Harbor. Hostilities ceased September 2, 1945, and by December 1945, the demobilization of U.S. forces had proceeded well along. To that date, December 1945, the U.S. government had spent $310 billion—$290 billion on the military—and had added $23 billion to the accounts that it maintained with the banks. To understand how substantial a sum $333 billion was for its day, we need but consider that for the four-year period as a whole, 1942-1945, U.S. national income came to just $770 billion. The WWII-era U.S. government, in other words, controlled 1.73 of those four years' national income.

By what financial means did the U.S. government take control of the 1.73 years' (90 weeks') national income? Taxation of the ordinary kind did 42 percent of the job (38 weeks' income), and the eight U.S. government bond drives did another 41 percent of it (37 weeks' income). The remaining 17 percent of the job (15 weeks' income), therefore, fell to the money-and-banking system, with the Federal Reserve at its head.

In April 1942, the Federal Reserve established a floor beneath which it wouldn't let the price of U.S. government bonds fall. Government bonds that the public wouldn't buy at that price, the Federal Reserve itself bought—$22 billion worth of them. The government's spending added that $22 billion to the banks' reserves. On net, however, bank reserves grew not by $22 billion but only by $3 billion, 21 percent, because the public withdrew $17 billion to use as pocket cash and the Federal Reserve canceled another $2 billion as foreign governments presented checks drawn against U.S. banks. Nevertheless, deposits doubled, growing by $38 billion. Apparently, the banks regarded government bonds, whose price the Federal Reserve supported, as being almost as good as cash and thus a close substitute for excess reserves that they had been holding before the war. Hence, the disproportionately large increase in checking account balances.

The total money stock, checking deposits plus pocket cash, grew by 115 percent, $55 billion, and all of it, not just the pocket cash, counts as government-issued money because—recall the fourth principle—on the banks' balance sheets, the new checking account balances stood opposite either cash reserves or government bonds. With the money-and-banking system's help, then, the government acquired goods worth $55 billion, roughly 15 weeks' income.[1] But how much of that real transfer should we write down to the public's voluntarily saving and how much should we write down to its having paid a tax on holding money balances?

The war years witnessed an extraordinary increase in annual U.S. real income. In fact, some estimates put real economic growth for the

---

1 Had the public's demand for money not risen (and its inverse, velocity, not fallen correspondingly) from its WWI-era level, the weeks' income figure would have about 40 percent lower.

period as high as 45 percent.[2] This feat meant more than just putting the Depression-era unemployed back to work; for by December 1941, when the United States declared war, the unemployment rate, upwards of 18 percent just three years earlier, had already fallen to 6 percent. The wartime economic expansion, furthermore, was unusual not just in its strength but also with respect to how much money the public wanted to hold relative to its increased income. Time and again, money holdings relative to annual income had fallen during cyclical economic expansions. During the WWII-era expansion, however, the ratio rose, by 30 percent.[3] The public desired a $42 {i.e., [.45 + .30 + (.45 x .30)] x $48} billion addition to its pre-war money holdings, then, and we should count that amount of new money, $42 billion, as evidence of voluntary saving.

The rest of the public's additional money holdings, $13 (i.e., $55 - $42) billion, we should count as evidence of forced saving and therefore as evidence of the public's having paid an implicit tax on holding the desired quantity of real money balances. To that $13 billion addition to its money balances, in other words, the public would have preferred goods. When the government spent $13 billion more new money, however, people had no choice but to accept the money, even though they had no intention of holding it. The $13 billion excess supply of money represented 14 percent of the $90 (i.e., $48 + $42) billion money stock demanded, and as the additional $13 billion got passed round and around, chasing goods that weren't any longer available, prices rose by roughly that percentage. A 14 percent higher price level threatened to reduce the public's real money holdings beneath the desired level and thus persuaded the public to absorb the $13 billion into nominal money balances demanded after all.[4]

---

2 For real income figures, see Louis D. Johnston and Samuel H. Williamson, "Annual Real and Nominal GDP for the Unites States, 1790 – Present", Economic History Services, October 2005, URL: http//www/eh.net/hmit/gdp/.

3 Producing durable consumers' goods – automobiles, electrical appliances, and the like – the very things that the public would have used to store wealth, was prohibited, and frustrated demand spilled over to financial assets, including money. Fear that an economic collapse and with it, eventually, lower prices would follow the war did its part, too, to increase the demand for money. See Milton Friedman and Anna J. Schwartz, *A Monetary History of the United States* (Princeton, N.J.: Princeton University Press, 1963), 580-60.

4 The 14 percent higher level of posted prices doesn't tell the whole story of wartime inflation. Faced with wage-and-price controls, some businesses raised prices indirectly. Methods included reducing the quality of goods and of the services provided with them, eliminating discounts, and if they had favorable price ceilings, shifting production to less desired goods. See Hugh Rockoff, *Drastic Measures: A History of Wage and Price Controls in the United States* (Cambridge: Cambridge University Press, 1984).

Counting $13 billion, nearly one quarter of total additional nominal money holdings, as evidence of the public's having paid an implicit tax on holding the desired quantity of real money balances means that, all told, taxation gave the U.S. government control over 42 weeks' WWII-era national income. Together, issuing bonds[5] and desired additions to the public's money holdings provided the government control over another 48 weeks' national income. Of the total, 90 weeks' national income, the government devoted 78 [i.e., ($290/$333) x 90] weeks' income to the war specifically. That number weeks' income, moreover, was just the original cost of the war. An additional cost, stemming from lost and physically impaired lives deserves consideration, as well. The additional cost proved quite substantial, even if calculated in coldly economic terms.

World War II cost the United States 364,000 brave lives, about .6 percent of its labor force. The war denied each of the military personnel killed what, on average, would have been a 40-year post-war working life. In effect, then, the United States lost a national income annuity that, in 1946, when national income was $223 billion, would have begun at $1.34 billion (i.e., .006 x $223) and that would have grown annually at roughly 8 percent. The business finance textbooks teach that, at a 5 percent interest rate, a 40-year annuity growing annually at 8 percent has present value equaling the first payment's present value – in this case, $1.34 billion/1.05, or $1.28 billion – times the factor 23. That product, about $29 billion, 8 weeks' income, requires some downward adjustment, however, because even if they had survived the war, some of the war dead would not have lived through the entire 40-year post-war period. The cost of caring for the more than 600,000 non-mortally wounded soldiers, on the other hand, offsets and probably exceeds that downward adjustment.

All in all, then, 80 weeks' worth of WWII-era income seems like a reasonable estimate of what it cost the United States to defeat Hitlerism and the related evils of its day. Victory came, but at a very high price. It's fortunate that the United States had both the will and the means to pay it. [6]

---

5 Government bonds that, on the banks' balance sheets stood as assets opposite passbook savings deposits and other liabilities, including government-owned deposits, not qualifying as actual money count as bonds held by the public.

6 I'll postpone until Chapter 12 considering whether one generation can shift even original costs to succeeding generations.

12

Two Cheers for the Government's Budget Deficit

The Production Possibilities Constraint

Just a single word sums up what the economist takes as the first and certainly most fundamental fact of life—fact of economic life, anyway—"scarcity". It's the old guns-and-butter argument. We can have some guns and *some* butter. But we can't have more guns and more butter. Later, perhaps, if through increased population and technological gains the economy grows, we can have more guns and more butter, but not today. The production possibilities constraint, as the textbooks call it, is the very benchmark of economic thinking. It shows that choices have to be made.

...Misapplied

Even benchmark thinking, however, can be misapplied. And the production possibilities constraint is misapplied, indeed, when economists use it to "prove" wrong anyone who thinks that, by having the government sell bonds to finance its spending, taxpayers can postpone or even avoid paying the government's bills. Take a WWII-era example to show how the supposed proof goes wrong.

The guns mounted on a U.S. naval destroyer launched in 1943 were 1943 guns. Then how could the economic burden of producing those guns have landed anywhere, one might ask, but on the shoulders of 1943 Americans? Weren't 1943 Americans the people who, to permit producing those guns, had less butter to enjoy? If so—and, of course, they were—then the no-shifting conclusion seems to follow.

The government issued debt to finance its 1943 military spending, debt that wouldn't come due until, say, 1973, yet it seems that 1943 Americans were the people on whose shoulders the real economic burden rested.

The argument appeals to the economist's instincts, harking back, as it does, to the production possibilities constraint and the lesson that its use teaches fledgling economists. *"Guns or butter, guns or butter—more of one means less of the other."* But the argument proves too much; a bond-financed budget deficit isn't just a tax called by another name. Of course, the guns aboard the 1943 destroyer were 1943 guns, and, of course, the resources used to make 1943 guns could have been used to produce 1943 butter. But *which* 1943 Americans went without their butter? The bondholders did, but—and this is James Buchanan's main point—they did so voluntarily.[1] They bought bonds, furthermore, not guns. If to have the bonds, these people had considered the required reduced butter consumption an undue burden, then they wouldn't have bought the bonds in the first place. Buying them was a choice entirely theirs to make.

No choice concerning paying their taxes, however, presented itself to postwar Americans. They *had* to pay their taxes, and with postwar tax revenues, the U.S. government made good on its wartime debt. Saying that the guns aboard the U.S. Navy destroyer were 1943 guns, then, doesn't at all establish the economic burden of providing the guns as having been a 1943 burden. That burden devolved upon postwar taxpayers. One generation of Americans can and, if this year's government spending is investment spending, which provides *long-term* benefits, perhaps even should shift the burden to the next generation.

Ricardian Non-Equivalence

Economists who rule out inter-generational burden shifting point to David Ricardo (*Principles of Political Economy and Taxation*, 1817) as their patron saint. But, actually, Ricardo cared very little about which generation shoulders the economic burden of government. He cared much more about the possibility that, by selling bonds to finance

---

1 James Buchanan, *Public Principles of Public Debt* (Homewood, Illinois: Richard D. Irwin, 1958), 48-72.

its spending, the government could leave the country with a smaller stock of real capital. Capital comes from saving. The people who buy government bonds do the saving; they set aside a portion of this year's crop, as it were, to plant as seed for next year's crop. If, instead of planting the seed, however, the government consumes it—dissaves, in other words—then there won't be much of a crop next year.

Whatever the government does with the seed that they've set aside, the government's creditors, of course, will insist on being repaid. Repaying them will mean levying new taxes. People might so clearly see the new taxes looming on the horizon, however, that they'd fully account for them in their personal finances today. To achieve their own personal financial goals, including goals concerning what they want to leave their heirs, people would then save even more than otherwise. Government spending would therefore entail no "fiscal burden", to use Ricardo's phrase; the economy's private capital stock would remain intact.

For Ricardo, this happy possibility existed—Ricardian equivalence, as it's now called—but only, and here to use Ricardo's words again, "in point of economy".[2] It existed, that is, as a piece of what, nowadays, we might call "blackboard economics". Real people, however, lack the foresight and perhaps even the concern to do the extra saving that it would take to leave the total private capital stock undiminished.

Ricardo wasn't a "Ricardian" at all. For the current generation of taxpayers, he didn't consider taxing and borrowing equally burdensome means of financing government spending. Ricardo urged taxation, which he felt people would pay not out of reduced saving but out of reduced consumption, as the preferable means of financing government spending.

Two Cheers for the Budget Deficit

Perhaps the government does spend too much. Still and all, people prefer government budget deficits to higher taxes; and when government spending is investment spending, not consumption spending, they do so for what one could argue is good reason. Two cheers, then, for the government's budget deficit.

---

2 See Gerald P. O'Driscoll, "The Ricardian Non-Equivalence Theorem", *Journal of Political Economy*, 1977, February, 207-10.

13

A Question for Tax Cutters

When I express doubt about a tax cut as a spending stimulus, I get looks of…well, to put it kindly, bemusement. What's wrong with this fellow? Didn't he say that he's an economist? Probably just to give me my comeuppance, they explain it for me. "If the government cuts taxes," they say, "then we'll keep more of what we make and, of course, we'll spend more." I can't argue with what they say. But I wonder…. Doesn't the tax cut leave the government with less to spend? Where's the *overall* stimulus, then? That's my question for tax cutters.

The tax cutters have their answer ready for me. Cutting taxes, they tell me, doesn't mean that the government actually has to cut its spending. The government can run a budget deficit—spend more, in other words, than it takes in through taxes—and finance its budget deficit by borrowing, by selling bonds. What the tax cutters say is true, but doesn't their answer mean that the people who buy the bonds will then have less to spend? Where's the *overall* stimulus? Again, that's my question for tax cutters.

But, again, the tax cutters have their answer ready for me. To finance its budget deficit, they say now, the government doesn't actually have to borrow: the government can just print money, however much money it needs to pay its bills. No argument there, of course. But doesn't this answer show that the spending stimulus that the tax cutters tout comes from an increased quantity of money, not from the tax cut itself? That's *really* my question for tax cutters.

14

What Does "The Market" Have To Do With It?

How Did the Market Do Today?

That's the cheery, late-afternoon greeting I get as I walk down the hall. (Have you ever noticed how it's always just "the market", never "the stock market", for anyone who wants to appear at all sophisticated in such matters?) I guess that, as an economist, I'm just supposed to *know* what "the market" did today. Not only that, but also why it did whatever it did, what it will do tomorrow, and what it all means for the unemployment figures due this week from the Labor Department. Irreverent though they may be, my answers, in order of question asked, are: (1) I don't know, (2) nobody knows, (3) if I knew, I wouldn't tell anyone, and (4) probably nothing. In connection with my irreverent answer #4, I offer the following little story.

Good Fairies and Bad

Suppose—just suppose—that the good fairy paid me a visit tonight and left a thousand shares of common stock under my pillow. I would wake to find myself feeling a lot wealthier than I felt the day before her visit. Could I spend more? Yes, I could. First, however, I would have to sell the stocks to get more of the medium of exchange. Cashiers at the stores will not accept stock certificates. They insist on money (or, if I use a credit card, a claim settled almost immediately in actual money).

Next, suppose that the good fairy bestowed her largesse not just upon me but upon all of us. Could we *all* spend more money? How could we if there's no more money to spend? Only if we individually decided to hold a smaller quantity of money *relative* to our incomes—only, that is, if the velocity of money rose—could the flow of spending and income expand.

Yes, the good fairy's Santa Claus-like visit might so inspire confidence that we would indeed be willing to get by with smaller real money balances. The reduced demand for holdings of money would tend to enlarge flows of spending and income. But, on the other hand, our increased wealth would make us feel that we could afford to hold *larger* real money balances. The increased demand for holdings of money would tend to shrink flows of spending and income. These two influences on the demand for money—the confidence effect and the wealth effect—besides tending to offset each other, would each probably be pretty small to begin with. They're not the main issue, anyway. The main issue is that, even when "the market" soars, the money supply doesn't have a dime added to it. Hence, my irreverent answer #4.

A stock market crash means that the fairy returns, not as a benefactor this time, however, but as a burglar. We'd all feel less wealthy upon awakening and quickly notice that things were missing. But that wouldn't mean that we'd collectively have less money to spend. The burglary—the stock market crash—wouldn't subtract anything, not even a dime, from the money supply. What about the demand for money holdings? Again, the effect on the demand for money is uncertain. The crash might cause us some anxiety and therefore make us want larger real money holdings than we had before. Now, however, feeling poorer after the crash, we might feel unable to afford holding even as large a real quantity of money as we had. The anxiety effect and its causing the demand for money to grow would tend to shrink spending flows and employment, but the negative wealth effect and its causing the demand for money to shrink would tend to expand them. Again, my irreverent answer #4.

The Importance of the Stock Market

None of this story is meant to say that the stock market is unimportant. The stock market is important. For the economist, however, its importance has much less to do with full employment than with capital formation.

Many of the people who came before us, even in the very best of their own times, were fully employed, more fully employed, in fact, than they wanted to be. Yet especially by our standards, they were very poor. These people couldn't afford to take a day off from work; their taking a day off from work would have meant a day with nothing to eat. Still, other people saved, and the stock market helped transform their saving into tools and machines. These tools and machines make our labors today more productive than they'd otherwise be, making it possible for many of us, including people who don't themselves actually own the tools and machines, to take a day off and still eat reasonably well.

15

October 6, 1979

The Announcement

A silver anniversary draws near. On October 6, 2004, 25 years will have passed since then Federal Reserve chief Paul Volcker made what people still call "The Announcement".[1] The Federal Reserve faced intense pressure to end the decade long U.S. inflation. Now, Mr. Volcker said, in conducting monetary policy, the Federal Reserve would de-emphasize interest rates. Instead, it would focus on the quantity of money, just as its monetarist critics, notably University of Chicago economist Milton Friedman, had long insisted it should. The change in the Federal Reserve's operating procedure would occur immediately.

The next few years proved difficult, indeed. The Reagan recession, as it came to be called, was the most severe U.S. recession since the recession of 1929-1933. Not, however, to any monetarist's surprise. The government's credibility—or, more exactly, its lack of credibility—was the problem. After the government's many unfulfilled promises to stop the inflation, yet another such promise carried very little weight. People just kept marking up prices and wages, even after the government had applied the monetary brakes. In real terms, then, the money supply wasn't big enough to keep business transactions going. Inflation had been bad enough. Now we had inflation *and* unemployment—stagflation, to use the newly coined term—and, supposedly, it was all monetarism's fault. In October 1982, the authorities declared the monetarist experiment over, done, a failure, and then ceremoniously laid the publicly disgraced doctrine to rest.

---

1 *Federal Reserve Bulletin*, October 1979, 830.

Monetarist Doctrine

Having wondered all along whether the Federal Reserve's declaration for monetarism had been more a public relations maneuver than a signal of substantive change, Yeager and I exhumed the body.[2] Before getting to the post mortem, however, let's review the doctrine itself.

Monetarism, first of all, draws a critical distinction between money's nominal and real quantities. By printing money and then using it to buy things or by selling things and then shredding the money that it receives for them, the Federal Reserve can make the nominal quantity of money, the actual number of dollars, however big or however small as it cares to make it. The public, however, through its habits concerning the spending or holding of money, determines the real quantity of money—the ratio, in other words, that the fixed number of dollars bears to the flow of spending and income per year.

Monetarists don't depict this ratio as an unchanging constant. The demand-for-money *function* relates the ratio to other variables, notably the interest rate. Because it makes holding money more costly, a higher interest rate makes the public desire a smaller ratio of money to income. But the community as a whole can't reduce the money-to-income ratio by getting rid of money. The money that I spend becomes yours, and the money that you spend becomes mine. We can pass money around more quickly, but its quantity doesn't change as a result. Instead, the unchanged nominal quantity of money becomes smaller as a fraction of the now expanded spending-and-income flow.

The nominal quantity of money is determined, then, on the supply side, the real quantity on the demand side. This distinction is what we *should* have found beneath the headstone reading "Monetarism, 1979-1982"...

The Post-Mortem

...but, upon exhuming the body, not at all what we found. The new operating procedure, first of all, began by taking the size of the spending-

---

2 Greenfield and Leland B. Yeager, "Money and Credit Confused: A Critique of Federal Reserve Doctrine and Procedure", *Southern Economic Journal*, 1986, 364-373, reprinted in George Selgin, ed., *The Fluttering Veil: Essays in Monetary Disequilibrium* by Leland B. Yeager (Indianapolis: Liberty Fund, 1997), 179-95. In his Federal Reserve Bank of Atlanta Distinguished Lecture, David Laidler ("Buffer Stock Money and the Transmission Mechanism," FRB of Atlanta *Economic Review*, 1987, March/April, 11-23) comes to the conclusion that Yeager and I reach.

and-income flow as a constant, an assumption that made any change in the nominal quantity of money a change in the real quantity, too. The new procedure asserted an inverse relationship, therefore, not just between the real quantity of money and the interest rate but also between the *nominal* quantity of money and the interest rate. Now, it's one thing to say, for example, that with income of $1,000 per year and seeing a 7 percent rate of interest, the public would want to hold a $100 money balance. It's altogether something different to say, however, that the Federal Reserve can itself establish 7 percent as the market rate of interest and that at the 7 percent interest rate, the nominal quantity of money will actually be $100. But that's exactly what the procedure said.

How was it supposed to happen? The Federal Reserve would choose $100, say, as its targeted quantity of checking account money. Then, holding income constant, it would solve the demand-for-money function, getting, let's assume again, 7 percent as the interest rate associated with the $100 money target. Against checking account money totaling $100, the banking system, facing a 10 percent reserve-requirement ratio, would need $10 of reserves. Through its open-market purchases of government bonds, however, the Federal Reserve would provide not $10 of reserves but, say, only $8.

The banks would then attempt to do what collectively, as a *system*, they couldn't do. They'd try to get the additional $2 of reserves by borrowing, from one another. They couldn't do it, because one bank's borrowing from another bank doesn't change the total quantity of reserves. According to the Federal Reserve's calculations, however, the banking system's attempting to borrow $2 from itself would push the inter-bank loan rate, the federal funds rate, up to the targeted rate, 7 percent. The gap between the 7 percent inter-bank rate and the Federal Reserve's, say, 4 percent discount rate would help the banks overcome their natural shyness about borrowing the required $2 of reserves from the Federal Reserve. The public, furthermore, at 7 percent interest, would sell to the banks promissory notes denominated $92, giving the banking system assets totaling $102—non-borrowed reserves of $8, borrowed reserves of $2, and borrowers' promissory notes denominated $92. The banking system's balance sheet would have to show liabilities also totaling $102—a promissory note reading "$2 due from banks to the Federal Reserve" and, right on money-supply target, checking accounts totaling $100.

Banking System				Federal Reserve		
Assets		Liabilities		Assets		Liabilities
Reserves	$10	Checking Accounts $100		Government Bonds $8		Banks' Deposits $10
Nonborrowed $8		Due to Federal		Due from Banks	2	
Borrowed 2		Reserve	2			
Loans	92					

A bull's eye…. On the dubious assumption that the demand for bank credit and the demand for holdings of bank money are the same thing, however, it was a bull's eye that couldn't be missed. The demand for bank credit (including the demand for Federal Reserve credit, i.e., the indirect borrowing that the public does by transferring to the Federal Reserve ownership of U.S. government bonds and that the banks do for the public when they borrow from the Federal Reserve) and the demand for holdings of bank money *aren't* the same thing. People who want to hold more bank money don't regard bank loans as the only way of getting the money. It would be a strange brand of monetarism that considered even the nominal quantity of money a demand-determined magnitude. According to monetarist thinking, major swings in total spending are caused by an imbalance between the actual quantity of money and the demanded quantity of money. How could the quantity of money affect total spending, at least according to monetarist thinking, if the quantity of money could never differ from the quantity that people want to hold?

Money and Credit Confused

Actually, and as any economist should understand, the demand for money and the demand for credit are different things altogether. The demand for money is a demand for holdings of the general medium of exchange. Though credit transactions involve money, the demand for credit is, at bottom, not a demand to hold money but, instead, a demand to hold somebody else's goods. Together with a limit on the existing quantity of money, the demand for money holdings determines the purchasing power of the monetary unit. Together with the supply of credit, the demand for credit determines the interest rate. The procedure unveiled on October 6, 1979, misidentified the demand for money with the demand for credit. The procedure therefore did what all interest-rate targeting schemes do. It picked up any change, increase or decrease, in the demand for credit and, in this case, by altering the banks' profit margin on reserves borrowed at the Federal Reserve's discount window, translated that change in the demand for credit into a same direction change in the quantity of money.

The October 6, 1979, procedure came with "reserves targeting" advertising, and the advertising made it sound like monetarism. Contrary to what a monetarist would recommend, however, the procedure didn't target total reserves. It "targeted", if that's the correctly used term here, just non-borrowed reserves. The procedure left borrowed reserves and thus total reserves and the money supply, as well, to change as the demand for credit changed, and in the same direction.

The Coroner's Verdict

Inter the body again. But this time, Mr. Volcker, please give the deceased a name other than "monetarism".

16

A "Dollar" That Would Really Mean Something

Something to Panic Over

In the video that accompanies Milton and Rose Friedman's "Anatomy of Crisis" (*Free to Choose*, 1978, Chapter 3), George Eccles gives an extremely vivid account of how his Salt Lake City bank weathered a Depression-era run on its holdings of Federal Reserve notes.

One morning, before opening the bank's door, Mr. Eccles saw a crowd gathering on the sidewalk. Recognizing the signs of a run, he called his tellers together. "Look," he told them firmly, "we can't let a line form at any of our windows. Work fast. Use big bills if you have them. No lunch breaks; you can have something at your station." The plan worked. The bank got through the first day.

When Eccles opened the bank's door the next day, he found the same size crowd waiting there to greet him. The bank's vault cash, Eccles knew all too well, had fallen to a dangerously low level. He expected an armored car delivery of cash that afternoon, but could the bank hold out that long? He wasn't sure.

Again, Eccles called his tellers together. This time, however, he told them that they should work very deliberately. "Even if the person who steps up to the window is your best friend, Joe Jones," he instructed the tellers, "ask him for identification. Use the smallest bills that you have in your till. Count the bills out very slowly—count them twice, maybe even three times. We have to make what little cash we have last until we get our shipment this afternoon." "*If* we get it," Eccles must have thought to himself.

All morning and into early afternoon, the tension grew. Then, at long last, the armored car pulled up outside the bank's door. The delivery men made their way through the crowd and into the bank. Eccles grabbed a sack of new bills in each hand and hoisted them up onto the counter. Then, he jumped up onto the counter himself and held the heavy sacks as high above his head as he could get them. "Look here," he announced as calmly as he possibly could. "We have cash, and there's plenty more where this came from." Soon, the clamor for cash ended, and the crowd broke up. The bank had survived the panic.

Up on that counter, holding the sacks of newly delivered bills above his head, Eccles reminds me of a surgeon who, having done an emergency at-home operation, holds a poisonous appendix aloft in his pincers and victoriously proclaims to the patient's much relieved family, "*Here's* our problem." The delivery of cash saved the Salt Lake City bank that day, true enough. The Federal Reserve note *itself*, however, the note's mere existence and use as our value unit, was and continues to be the money-and-banking system's real problem, its poisonous appendix. For one thing, banks have no choice but to keep checking account money convertible into the Federal Reserve note, yet they face an almost irresistible incentive to hold just fractional reserves of it. The combination makes the banks vulnerable to runs.

The surgeon's patient will survive without the appendix; of that much, we can be reasonably sure. But could *our* patient, the U.S. economy, get along without the Federal Reserve note? Leland Yeager and I say that it could and, what's more, with important though little recognized advantages that merely insuring deposits or even altogether outlawing fractional-reserve banking just couldn't deliver.[1]

Yards and Yardsticks, Dollars and Dollarsticks

The Federal Reserve note is our existing monetary system's potentially fatal flaw. But the Federal Reserve note is so much a part *of* the existing system that most of us don't even see it as a flaw, let alone a potentially fatal flaw.

---

1   See Greenfield and Leland B. Yeager, "A Laissez-Faire Approach to Monetary Stability", *Journal of Money, Credit, and Banking*, 1983, August, 302-15 and also "Can Monetary Disequilibrium be Eliminated?" (followed by Allan Meltzer's "Comment"), Cato Journal, Fall 1989, 405-19; both articles are reprinted in George Selgin, ed., *The Fluttering Veil: Essays in Monetary Disequilibrium by Leland B. Yeager* (Indianapolis: Liberty Fund, 1997). The scheme discussed here bears a family resemblance to Irving Fisher's compensated-dollar plan. See Chapter 10 here and Don Patinkin, "Indirect Convertibility and Irving Fisher's Compensated-Dollar", *Journal of Money, Credit, and Banking*, 1996, February, 139-31.

An analogy will help bring the economy's little recognized fatal flaw into sharper focus. Imagine telling our carpenters that, although they have a lot of measuring to do today, they shouldn't worry about getting themselves more yardsticks. They won't need more yardsticks, imagine telling the carpenters, because we'll have the meaning of the word "yard" changed and, by doing so, enable each of the yard*sticks* that they already have to do more measuring. Yes, the General Convention on Weights and Measure defines the "yard" as the distance that light in a vacuum travels every (.9144/299,792,458) seconds, but that's no problem; considering the increased demand for yardsticks, we'll have the travel time cut, say, in half, to (.4572/299,792,458) seconds. The light will travel just half as far as it did before, and each existing yardstick will therefore measure twice as many "yards" as it did before. "Absurd", you would say. "What kind of measuring unit could, for its very meaning, depend on the demand for the tool that we do the measuring with?"

"What *kind* of measuring unit?" you ask. The "dollar", that's what kind. "Dollar", our unit of account, means the changeable, supply-anddemand-determined value of the system's dominant medium of exchange, the Federal Reserve note. Lacking the sanctity that we accord the "yard", the "dollar" has to undergo redefinition until the existing physical quantity of the medium of exchange—dollarsticks, if you will—satisfies the public's demand for holdings of it. When there are too few dollarsticks to go around, the required change in the meaning of "dollar" occurs painfully and slowly, through a general deflation of spending and, eventually, prices.

Our existing monetary system, in other words, gives the medium of exchange priority over the unit of account. The Federal Reserve note actually defines the unit of account: a dollar bill *is* the unit that we call a "dollar". Surely, if it would be absurd to have the yardstick define the unit of length, then having the medium of exchange define the unit of account is even more absurd. The quantity of a unit-of-account-defining medium of exchange can get out of line with the demand for holdings of it, and eliminating such an imbalance requires changing the very meaning of the unit of account. Its meaning can't change, however, except by disrupting exchanges on ordinary markets and thereby jeopardizing output and employment.

But suppose that there were no Federal Reserve note, no government-issued, dominant medium of exchange, whose value had to change, however sluggishly and painfully, because barring adroit policy manipulations, its quantity couldn't change. Suppose, too, that the "dollar" (or perhaps, for convenience of arithmetic scale, 1,000 "dollars") were defined as the value of a collection of goods and services so comprehensive as to make the general price level expressed in that unit stable, practically by definition. And, finally, suppose that private firms issued media of exchange—not just transferable deposits but notes, too—denominated in the stable-by-definition unit of account.

These issuers wouldn't be banks, not in the sense that we know them these days. Issuers of media of exchange denominated in the stable-by-definition unit of account wouldn't be called upon, as banks are everyday, to convert their notes and deposits into an even more basic medium of exchange; no medium of exchange more basic than their own would exist. Issuers wouldn't be vulnerable to a 1930s-style bank run because there wouldn't be anything to run *for*.

Still, competition would force issuers to make good their promises, as stated, for example, on the 100-dollar notes themselves; the notes would actually say "100 dollars". Because convertibility directly into the actual dollar-defining comprehensive collection of goods and services would be impossible, however, convertibility would have to be indirect. Anyone issuing a 100-dollar note or transferable deposit, in other words, would have to keep it convertible into the changeable quantity of some agreed redemption medium, probably high-grade securities, that at prevailing market prices was actually *worth* 100 of the dollar-defining goods-andservices bundles. The great bulk of such redemptions would take place not "over the counter" but through the clearinghouses, as rival issuers, in the ordinary course of business, gained possession of one another's notes and deposits and then sent them through for payment.

Attentive people would thwart any threat that the unit of account might pose of prying itself loose from the bundle of goods and services defining it. Though things could hardly get anywhere near this far, say that the unit-defining bundle's composite price rose toward two thousand dollars, for example, because people wanted to reduce their holdings of exchange media and wanted to do so by buying goods. In this far-fetched circumstance, you could do better with a note or a deposit denominated 100 dollars than just spend it on goods and services. You could take the 100-dollar note or deposit back to the issuer, instead, and, in exchange, get securities that you could sell for notes and deposits denominated 200 dollars. Then, you could turn those notes and deposits in for redemption property worth 400 dollars and keep right on going. Your eagerness (and everyone else's eagerness, too, of course) to get notes and deposits not to spend but to present for redemption would tend to bring the bundle's composite price back down to 1,000 dollars. Arbitrage incentives would thus trigger powerful, corrective forces. They would keep the unit of account from losing contact with its commodity-bundle definition in the first place while shrinking the supply of exchange media to keep it in line with the public's shrunken demand for holdings of them.

Probably, only specialists, working under the auspices of the clearinghouses, would engage in arbitrage and thus work to keep the unit of account from losing touch with its comprehensive physical definition. Even these specialists, however, wouldn't have to know anything about how the system as a whole worked; the workings of the system as a whole would be something for economists to study. Carpenters, arbitrage specialists, and even economists would go about their personal business just as they do nowadays, using notes and checks denominated in "dollars".

If the public wanted to hold a larger quantity of notes and deposits, then the composite price of the bundle would begin to show signs of dipping beneath 1,000 dollars. Issuers of notes and deposits would then have a very strong incentive to issue more of them. Issuers would see that, even if called on to redeem a 100-dollar note or deposit, they could do so with redemption media purchasable for something less than 100 dollars. The profit motivated expansion of notes and deposits to satisfy the public's strengthened demand for holding them would keep the bundle's composite price from dipping beneath 1,000 dollars in the first place. Again, the unit of account would adhere to its physical definition.

Conclusion

Having private issuers of notes and deposits hitch onto a unit of account defined not as the value of a government-issued medium of exchange but, instead, as the value of a comprehensive bundle of goods and services would eliminate macroeconomic instability. No longer, even if only sluggishly and therefore with painful side effects, would the whole price level have to adjust because a policy blunder had made the quantity of money too small. Instead, the quantity of exchange media would adjust itself to demand automatically, and at the stable-by-definition price level. The "dollar" would have the same desirable priority over any particular issuer's medium of exchange that the "yard" has over any particular manufacturer's yardstick. The "dollar", in other words, would really mean something.

17

Some American Monetary Hoztory

Prologue

L. Frank Baum's *The Wonderful Wizard of Oz* ranks among the all-time popular children's stories. But it may be something else, too—an allegory of its very troubled age, the American 1890s. Building on earlier such interpretations of the story, Hugh Rockoff, who speaks here through italicized print, has solved several of its monetary mysteries and, by so doing, has made this story one of my classroom favorites.[1]

To Oz

Baum's story begins in Kansas, of course, where Dorothy, a young farm girl, lives with her Auntie Em and Uncle Henry. *Dorothy represents America—honest, kindhearted, and plucky.* A cyclone carries the farmhouse off to Oz, *a land in which an ounce of gold has almost mystical significance.* The cyclone stands for the late nineteenth-century Populist movement in American politics. A reaction to the country's depressed economic conditions, Populism diagnosed the depression of the 1890s as essentially a monetary problem: too little gold. *The Populist movement came roaring out of the West in 1896, shaking the political establishment to its very foundations.*

The whirling farmhouse lands with a thud, right smack atop the Wicked Witch of the East. Now, of the Wicked Witch of the East, nothing remains but a pair of silver slippers. When Dorothy and her little dog, Toto, scramble safely from the farmhouse, the Munchkins

---

1 Hugh Rockoff, "The Wizard of Oz as a Monetary Allegory", *Journal of Political Economy*, 1990, August, 739-60.

greet them and then summon the Good Witch of the North. She makes the silver slippers Dorothy's, as a gift.

Silver, as represented by Dorothy's slippers, was the key Populist issue. Mostly farmers, Populists wanted the U.S. mint to buy silver in unlimited quantities and, what's more, wanted the mint, again, as it had long before, to use just16 times as much silver in striking a dollar coin as it would use gold. In 1896, the 16:1 ratio would have required the mint to pay $1.29 for an ounce of silver, a price nearly twice what the silver miners, whom Populists had little difficulty, of course, recruiting to their cause, were then getting for their metal. From the world over, silver would flow to the U.S. mint. Free coinage of silver at 16: 1 would enlarge the U.S. money supply and therefore, Populists argued, cure the country's economic ills.

Buttons courtesy of Ron Wade Buttons and Norm Steiner Collection.

William Jennings Bryan (L), (Nebraska) and Arthur Sewall (R), (Maine), the 1896 Democratic Party Ticket, "Free Silver and Free Trade"

At the Democrats' 1896 nominating convention, Nebraska congressman William Jennings Bryan, then but a minor player on the national political stage, became the living embodiment of the free silver movement. "You shall not press down upon the brow of labor a crown of thorns. You shall not crucify mankind upon a cross of gold", declared Bryan that July day in Chicago. The sweltering convention hearkened to Bryan's clarion call, bestowing upon the Great Commoner, as Bryan would become known among the faithful, the nomination that incumbent president Grover Cleveland could well have regarded as, by right, his own.

Now dead, the Wicked Witch of the East represents President Grover Cleveland, who, in reaction to the Panic of 1893, led the repeal of the Sherman Silver Purchase Act of 1890. The act, though it stopped short of free coinage, had pledged the U.S. government to purchase 4.5 million ounces of silver per month at market price and, according to the anti-silver people, had caused the 1893 panic by casting doubt on the U.S. government's commitment to the gold standard. When incumbent Cleveland and his pro-gold Democrats went down to defeat at the party's 1896 convention, America could vote for Bryan and free silver. *But the American people, like the munchkins, never understood the power that was theirs once the Wicked Witch was dead.* The "sound money" candidate, Republican William McKinley, defeated Bryan in 1896 and would defeat him again in 1900.

Buttons courtesy of Norm Steiner Collection.

William McKinley (L), (Ohio) and Garret A. Hobart (R), (New Jersey), the 1896 Republican Party Ticket, "Sound Money and Protection"

In fact, Bryan would lose yet a third time, in 1908, when he ran against another Republican from Ohio, William Howard Taft. Nevertheless, Bryan judged himself a success. Many of the reforms that he championed, including prohibition, female suffrage, a progressive income tax, and labor's right to organize, became realities in his America. And for his successes, Bryan never hesitated to credit the Democratic Party.

Not even after it had turned against him would Bryan forsake the Democratic Party.[2] In 1920, for example, when the Prohibition Party

---

2 On Bryan's devotion to the Democratic Party, see Lawrence W. Levine, *Defender of the Faith: William Jennings Bryan; the Last Decade, 1915-1925* (New York: Oxford University

offered him its presidential nomination, Bryan declined. He declined even though he considered prohibition a moral calling and even though the Prohibition Party espoused not just prohibition but various other reforms that Bryan had championed. *Toto stands for the Prohibition Party, "Toto" being a takeoff on the word "teetotaler".*

The Yellow Brick Road

The Munchkins can't get Dorothy and Toto back to Kansas. Neither can The Good Witch of the North. The Witch, however, urges Dorothy to follow the yellow brick road. *The road is a symbol of the gold standard. Following it will lead to the Emerald City (Washington, D.C.).* There, she'll find the Wizard, and from the Wizard, the Good Witch tells Dorothy, she and Toto might get the help that they need. The Witch gives Dorothy a protective kiss on the forehead and then sends her and the little dog on their way.

Soon after setting out along the yellow brick road, Dorothy and Toto happen upon a dejected scarecrow having very little success keeping the hungry crows out of the cornfield that he's supposed to be guarding. Dorothy helps him down from his uncomfortable perch. Pointing to his head, the scarecrow shows Dorothy that where he should have a brain he has nothing but straw. *The scarecrow is the western farmer.* Encouraged by the eastern establishment to doubt his own intelligence, he should just tend his fields and leave to the experts the thorny question of choosing a monetary standard. Dorothy can't very well abandon the poor scarecrow! She insists that he accompany her and Toto to the Emerald City. Once they reach the Emerald City, the Wizard will give the scarecrow a brain Perhaps the farmer will come to see the monetary question as having much less to it than the experts would have him believe.[3]

As Dorothy, Toto, and now the Scarecrow make their way optimistically along the yellow brick road, the Tin Woodman awaits

---

Press, 1965).

3 *This attitude is best illustrated in the leading tract of the free silver movement, W.B. Harvey's* Coin's Financial School. *The imaginary Coin is a small boy who conducts a series of lectures in Chicago attended by…Lyman Gage, a Chicago banker who became secretary of the Treasury, and James Laurence Laughlin, a professor of economics at the University of Chicago. Although first contemptuous of the untutored boy, they gradually find their arguments for a gold standard refuted.* In Coin's Financial Fool, *Horace White answered Harvey. Both Coin tracts are reprinted in Paul Samuelson and Herman Kroos, eds.,* Documentary History of Banking and Currency in the United States, *Chelsea House, 1969.*

them. The Tin Woodman began as flesh and blood. His axe would take flight, however, and each time it took flight, do him bodily harm. The tinsmith made the Woodman whole again, but now, after repeated mishaps and repairs made necessary by them, he's entirely tin and, what's even worse perhaps, his joints are so badly rusted that he can't work. *He has joined the ranks of those unemployed in the depression of the 1890s, a victim of the unwillingness of the eastern goldbugs to countenance an increase in the stock of money through the addition of silver.*

Dorothy gives the Tin Woodman a shot of oil, which gets him moving again (monetary lubrication for the ailing economy?). Owing to his most recent injury and what the tinsmith had to do to repair him yet again, however, the Woodman has another problem: he lacks a heart. *Industrialization has alienated the workingman, turning an independent artisan into a mere cog in a giant machine.* Dorothy insists that the Tin Woodman, too, come along to see the Wizard. If the Wizard can get Dorothy and Toto back to Kansas and can give the Scarecrow a brain, why there's no reason at all to think that the Wizard can't give the Tin Woodman a heart.

The cowardly lion, William Jennings Bryan himself, is last to join Dorothy and her band of travelers. *The sequence is not accidental. The populist movement was started by the western farmers, was joined by the workingman (but only to a limited extent, as shown by the failure of the Lion's claws to make an "impression" on the Tin Woodman), and then was joined by Bryan. The roaring lion is a good choice for one of the greatest American orators.* But why a cowardly lion? In 1898, Bryan had spoken clearly against fighting a war with Spain, but to no avail. War fever had the country firmly in its grip. Though Bryan, with much fanfare, eventually accepted a commission as colonel in the Nebraska state militia, the Republicans hadn't forgotten his anti-war speeches. Besides being a latecomer to the cause, furthermore, Bryan hadn't actually made it all the way to Cuba and the battlefield, but only to the Florida Everglades, where he and his military unit took their training.

The Republicans branded him cowardly, but then so, too, did some of his former supporters. *It was obvious almost immediately after the 1896 election that Bryan would be the standard bearer again in 1900. But with the return of prosperity, he received advice to soft pedal silver and to concentrate on new issues such as anti-imperialism and opposition to the trusts. After the Spanish-American War, the United States, to retain control of the Philippines, put down a bloody rebellion. The populists opposed fighting to hold the Philippines. But many populists feared that Bryan would push this issue to the exclusion of silver. They considered this line of action pure cowardice.* With Dorothy's assurance that the Wizard will give him courage, the lion joins the expedition; and off they go – *the little party reminds me of Coxey's "army", which in 1894 marched on Washington, D.C., seeking redress of economic grievances* – traveling the yellow brick road again.

Before they reach the Emerald City, the travelers meet several challenges, and each displays the trait that he sees himself as somehow lacking. When the lion falls asleep in the deadly poppy field, however, they require assistance. *The poppy field is another reference to the dangers of putting anti-imperialism ahead of silver. Bryan's Populist advisors were concerned that if he failed to stress the issues of greatest concern to rank-and-file Populists, particularly silver, he would fail to win their support. It is therefore appropriate that field mice, little people concerned with everyday issues, pull the Cowardly Lion from the Deadly Poppy Field.*

The Emerald City

At long last, Dorothy and her little group reach the Emerald City. Though the Guardian of the Gate has no doubt that the Wizard can help them, they can't see him until morning. Meanwhile, just to enter the city, they'll each have to put on green-tinted eyeglasses, held fast to the wearer's head by a gold buckle. *The conservative financiers who run the Emerald City force its citizens to look at the world through money colored glasses.* Gold, of course, holds the whole monetary system together.

Dorothy and her fellow travelers must stay overnight in the Emerald Palace. Taking Dorothy to her room, the Guardian leads her through seven dimly lighted corridors and up three rickety staircases. *It is not surprising that the layout of the Emerald Palace should reflect the numbers seven and three. The Crime of '73 was a crucial event in populist monetary history. Legislation that year eliminated the coinage of the silver dollar.* In 1873, the public had taken but scant notice of the "crime" because miners of silver were getting a better price on the commercial market than they could get at the U.S. mint.[4] The 1890s depression changed

---

4 Although there was no actual "crime of 1873", influential members of government were nevertheless interested in seeing that, when the paper dollar again became convertible into a precious metal, as would happen on January 1, 1879, the precious metal should be

things, however, and miners, who now couldn't find a good market for their silver, turned to the mint. The mint's refusing to buy the metal gave Populists further evidence of "the conspiracy against silver".

The depression of the 1890s threw a harsh light on the miners' situation, and morning, when it comes in the Emerald City, throws an equally harsh light on Dorothy's. The Wizard agrees to see Dorothy and her little troupe, but only individually, not together, and though he presents himself alike to no two of them, for each petitioner he has the very same answer. The Wizard's answer is plain and simple. I can help you, the Wizard says, but, before I do, you'll have to do something for me.

Who is this Wizard who speaks through various figureheads and adheres to such a Republican view of the world? To a populist, there was only one answer: Marcus Alonzo Hanna. He was the brains behind McKinley and his campaign. The money that Hanna raised from giant corporations, according to the Populists, defeated Bryan. During the campaign, Hanna urged people to visit McKinley in Ohio, where each day, from his front porch, he would extol Republican virtues, namely, the virtues of sound money and protection. *If Cleveland was the Wicked Witch of the East, slain in 1896, McKinley in 1896 and 1900 was the very much alive Wicked Witch of the West.* The Wizard wants the Wicked Witch of the West dead; those are his terms.

The Witch won't succumb easily. She has the Golden Cap, which allows whoever holds it three wishes. With the first wish, the Witch has already banished the Wizard to the East, and with the second wish, she has enslaved the yellow Winkies. With the Witch's enslavement of the Winkies and though in a way that sounds condescending to the modern ear, Baum makes *reference to McKinley's deciding to deny the Philippines immediate independence after the war with Spain and to make them a U.S. territory instead.* Two of the Wicked Witch's three wishes have already been spent.

The third wish, however, remains for her to use. With it, she calls down the winged monkeys, commanding them to attack Dorothy and the rest. *The Winged Monkeys represent the Plains Indians, free*

---

gold, not silver. See Milton Friedman, "The Crime of 1873", *Journal of Political Economy*, 1990, December, 1159-94, reprinted in Friedman, *Money Mischief, Episodes in Monetary History* (New York: Harcourt Brace & Co., 1992), 51-79 and also Greenfield and Hugh Rockoff, "Yellowbacks out West and Greenbacks back East: Social Choice Dimensions of Monetary Reform", *Southern Economic Journal*, 1996, April, 902-15.

spirits brought low by the relentless western march of the frontier and the overarching power of the gold standard. But the winged monkeys don't dare harm Dorothy herself. They see on her forehead the mark of the Good Witch's kiss, and they fear the power of Good even more than they fear the Wicked Witch herself. They'll do no more than deposit Dorothy at the evil one's castle.

Neither will the Wicked Witch do Dorothy harm; for she, too, fears the power of Good. Desperate, however, to have the power of the silver slippers, the Witch trips Dorothy and snatches one of them away. Now divided, the silver slippers are powerless. *This refers to McKinley's position on silver: bimetallism should be reestablished but only after an international agreement on it. He argued that an international agreement would raise the world demand for silver sufficiently to prevent the United States from being flooded with silver. The Populists believed that this was merely so much talk.* Greatly angered, Dorothy pours a bucket of water over the Witch, who then, before Dorothy's very eyes, melts away to nothing.

The Wizard Unmasked

With the Wicked Witch of the West dead, Dorothy and her friends make their way back to the Emerald City, expecting the Wizard to keep his part of their deal. While with great expectations the party stands waiting in the Wizard's chamber, Toto escapes Dorothy's clutches, grabs a corner of the curtain shielding the Wizard from view, and then pulls the whole curtain back. The Wizard isn't a wizard at all, they can all see plainly, but just an elderly, white-haired man with a special effects machine. In the Emerald City, as in Washington, D.C., everything is smoke and mirrors.

Though much embarrassed, the "Wizard" still has a few tricks left up his sleeve. With some ordinary household knickknacks, he solves three of the problems—bran and pins for the Scarecrow's brain; a silk lined heart, filled with sawdust, for the Tin Woodman's heart; and for the Cowardly Lion, courage in the form of a green liquid. Only Dorothy and Toto remain. How can he get them back to Kansas? A hot air balloon! That's it! To get them back to Kansas, he'll use a hot air balloon. Hurriedly, he and Dorothy make their preparations. When time comes for them to depart Oz, the bands are playing and all the munchkins are cheering.

As the balloonists wave their good-byes from the gondola, however, Toto spots something. The dog leaps out of the basket to give chase, and Dorothy, ever loyal Dorothy, follows him. Quickly, she collars the dog and heads back to the balloon. But it's too late. The balloon has broken lose of its mooring, leaving Dorothy and Toto behind, stranded forever, it seems, in the land called Oz.

The Power of Silver

Dorothy has one last hope. She must find Glinda, the Good Witch of the South. *The South was generally sympathetic to free silver, so it is not surprising that it is ruled by a good witch.* Glinda has the answer for Dorothy—to get herself and Toto back to Kansas, she need only click together the heels of her silver slippers three times. *The power to solve her problems (by adding silver to the money stock) had been there all the time.* Dorothy—America, that is—had simply failed to recognize the power of silver.

The Gold Standard Act of 1900 resolved the long-standing and often very bitter monetary controversy once and for all, and in favor of gold. The Populists' dream, free silver, never became a reality. Even so, Bryan found vindication in the turn-of-the century economic recovery. Discoveries of new gold fields, together with a newly invented chemical process, the cyanide process, for more cheaply extracting gold from ore, had caused significant growth of the money supply. Gold, not silver, had relieved the economy's monetary constraint, true. But its having been gold and not silver to break the monetary constraint made little difference to Bryan. Too small a money supply had caused America's economic problems, and an infusion of money had cured them.

The Baum Debate

Rockoff's "The Wizard of Oz as a Monetary Allegory" has touched off a lively debate, conducted in the pages of the *Baum Bugle* and elsewhere, concerning author Baum. Did Baum have strong political leanings? Did he really use his *The Wonderful Wizard of Oz* to express them? *Baum left no hard evidence that he intended his story to have allegorical meaning: no diary entry, no letter, not even an offhand remark to a friend.* Even so, some writers peg Baum as a dyed-in-the-wool Democrat, a true silverite.

Other writers, however, peg him as an ingenious Republican, who through thinly veiled parody, sought to belittle the free silver movement. To help establish Baum's Republican credentials, these writers point to a poem that, just shortly after the Democrats' 1896 convention adjourned, Baum wrote for a staunchly Republican newspaper, the *Chicago Times-Herald*. Baum gave his poem the title "When McKinley Gets the Chair".

"When McKinley Gets the Chair"
by L. Frank Baum

When McKinley gets the chair, boys,
There'll be a jollification
Throughout our happy nation
And contentment everywhere!
Great will be our satisfaction
When the "honest money" faction
Seats McKinley in the chair.

No more ample crops of grain
That in our granaries have lain
Will seek a purchaser in vain
Or be at the mercy of the "bull" or the "bear"
Our merchants won't be trembling
At the silverites' dissembling
When McKinley gets the chair!

When McKinley gets the chair, boys,
The magic word "protection"
Will banish all dejection
And free the workingman from every care;
We will gain the world's respect
When it knows our coin's "correct"
And McKinley's in the chair.

Those writers who would make Baum a Democrat, of course, interpret his *Times-Herald* poem as something other than a sincere Republican's manifesto of sound money and protectionism. They interpret the poem as calculated irony. In a "coin that's 'correct'", they say, Baum saw anything but financial rectitude, and in "the magic word 'protection'", Baum saw economic ruin.

The Baum debate goes on, then.[5] Even some of the author's descendants have weighed in, insisting that *The Wonderful Wizard of Oz* is exactly what, in its preface, Baum described the book as being, a story that he had written for no reason other than "to please children of today".

Epilogue

• President William McKinley in 1901 fell victim to an assassin's bullet.

• Marcus Hanna in 1897 took the senate seat left empty when John Sherman of Ohio resigned to become President McKinley's secretary of the treasury. Hanna then won election for a full Senate term. He died in 1904, a leading candidate for the Republican presidential nomination.

• William Jennings Bryan in 1913 became President Woodrow Wilson's secretary of state. Declaring that Germany had the right to protect itself against ships carrying arms to the Allies, Bryan resigned in 1915 rather than approve Wilson's second written protest over its having sunk the Lusitania. Bryan campaigned for strict U.S. neutrality but, when America joined the Allies in 1916, volunteered to serve. In 1925, he argued Tennessee's case against a high school teacher who, encouraged by his local school board, had violated the state law against teaching Darwin's theory of evolution. Depicted in the play (and later motion picture) "Inherit the Wind", the case became known, after the defendant, as the Scopes Monkey Trial. Bryan won the case—for the record, anyway. After having combatively interrogated Bryan himself as a witness, opposing counsel, the legendary Clarence Darrow, stipulated the facts of the case as Bryan had earlier presented

---

5 For citations and anti-allegory commentary, see Bradley A. Hansen, "The Fable of the Allegory: *The Wizard of Oz* in Economics", *Journal of Economic Education*, 2002, Summer, 254-65.

them. Darrow thus denied Bryan the chance to deliver his much awaited closing argument and then, on appeal, to challenge the state law's constitutionality. The court found Scopes guilty, and he paid a $100 fine. Five days later, when the Commoner, born in 1865, passed from the scene, an era came to a close.

www.ingramcontent.com/pod-product-compliance
Lightning Source LLC
Chambersburg PA
CBHW030853180526
45163CB00004B/1554